simply WOOD

simply WOOD

40 stylish and easy-to-make projects for the modern woodworker

ROSHAAN GANIEF

Fox Chapel
PUBLISHING

dedication

To Elsa, for your enduring spirit.

acknowledgments

Thanks to all my family and friends, who have believed in me and my craft since day one. Your unconditional support and motivational words have given me the stepping stones to reach higher than I possibly could on my own.

A special thanks to my grandma (Mamma), the strongest woman I know. Your strength is truly an inspiration to me every day. I love you, Mamma.

Thanks to Marvin Marshall, my favorite landlord, who gave me a start by providing me the space to make as much sawdust as I possibly could. You will always be special to me.

Thanks to Martica Jilek, who has always been gracious enough to lend a hand, no matter how mundane the task. You are such a trooper for enduring all the grunt work.

Thanks to Cam Russell and Ken Guenter, my extremely talented and exceptionally knowledgeable instructors at Camosun College, for giving me invaluable professional skills to succeed in life.

Thanks to everyone at Fox Chapel, with a special thanks to Peg Couch, who saw potential and made this book happen.

Finally, a very special thanks to Elsa Chu, the true backbone of this project. Thanks for the many hours invested in great step-by-step photography, typing out (definitely not my strong suit) my pencil scribbles, proofreading, and keeping everything organized. I will always be indebted to you!

© 2010 by Roshaan Ganief and Fox Chapel Publishing Company, Inc.

Simply Wood is an original work, first published in 2010 by Fox Chapel Publishing Company, Inc. The patterns contained herein are copyrighted by the author. Readers may make copies of these patterns for personal use. The patterns themselves, however, are not to be duplicated for resale or distribution under any circumstances. Any such copying is a violation of copyright law.

All step-by-step photography by Elsa Chu.

ISBN 978-1-56523-440-6

Library of Congress Cataloging-in-Publication Data

Ganief, Roshaan.
 Simply wood : 40 stylish and easy-to-make projects for the modern woodworker / Roshaan Ganief.
    p. cm.
 Includes bibliographical references and index.
 ISBN 978-1-56523-440-6 (alk. paper)
 1. Woodwork. I. Title.
 TT180.G35 2010
 684'.08--dc22

                          2010021942

To learn more about the other great books from Fox Chapel Publishing, or to find a retailer near you, call toll-free 800-457-9112 or visit us at *www.FoxChapelPublishing.com*.

Note to Authors: We are always looking for talented authors to write new books in our area of woodworking, design, and related crafts. Please send a brief letter describing your idea to Acquisition Editor, 1970 Broad Street, East Petersburg, PA 17520.

Printed in China
First printing: October 2010

preface

I appreciate art in many forms and mediums. I especially love art that is tactile, interactive, and best of all, functional. For this reason, I have a deep love for working with wood and producing pieces of functional art for everyday living. I get genuine pleasure and satisfaction out of seeing someone appreciate my work by using it every day.

This book is filled with 40 such projects, which are not only fun to make, but also very satisfying. I will be demonstrating 20 of these projects in a photographed step-by-step format; I've also included an alternative pattern that can easily be substituted for each one. Most of the patterns can also be easily modified into other projects. For example, you may want a set of home accessories that all have the orchid motif. Even though the only orchid motif patterns in this book are the photo frame, lamp, and tissue box, by simply enlarging or shrinking the pattern on a photocopier, or

tweaking a line here or there, you can end up with wall art, coasters, candle holders, and more. The possibilities are endless.

You will also notice I concentrate on a few themes that are interwoven throughout the book. I have designs for people who appreciate Asian aesthetics, designs for those who love botanical motifs, some for all those geometric-shape enthusiasts, and some sentimental designs, just to name a few. You will surely have a great base to create many sets of items with many themes.

I have kept the woodworking easy enough for the beginner, but have also kept the more advanced scrollers and woodworkers in mind by including some exciting and fun projects to tackle. I am sure there will be something for everyone in this book—I know that I had a great time making all the projects on these pages. I am very excited about the opportunity to share my designs with you. Have fun!

—Roshaan Ganief

contents

Chapter 4: Wall Accents

Chapter 5: Office Accessories

Appendix

about the author

My name is Roshaan Ganief. I grew up in the beautiful, scenic city of Cape Town, South Africa. I moved to Canada with my family when I was 17 years old in the hopes that I would have a chance at a brighter future. Many doors opened suddenly that had been shut for me in the past.

I have always known from a very young age that I would follow an artistic path in whatever career I chose. With that in mind, I pursued a career in Fine Art and Design. I soon realized that my art not only had to be beautiful, but also had to be functional.

Eight years ago, I stumbled upon the fascinating medium of woodworking during my exploration of different mediums, which also included ceramics, printmaking, and sculpture. I was soon hooked on this new and wonderful medium. I love the natural characteristics of wood and how working with wood is both challenging and extremely rewarding. A few years later, I discovered the scroll saw and fell in love instantly. The synergy for my passion of woodworking and my love of art and design is what you will see in these pages.

Choosing that path has manifested itself in many interesting ways since then. I have collaborated with a very talented metal artist, with whom I made custom tea boxes and various home décor items out of wood; participated in various juried craft shows; displayed my work in cafes and galleries (including a solo show at a local Vancouver gallery); donated artwork to a great hospital fundraising auction; and opened a business.

I taught myself as much as I could about this amazing medium, but knowing that there is never an end to learning, I sought out experts who knew more about wood.

I attended the Fine Furniture Program at Camosun College, a school located in the picturesque city of Victoria in British Columbia. Shortly after finishing the manuscript for this book, I graduated from the program and received a certificate in Fine Furniture, as well as a certificate in Joinery Foundation.

Today, I am proud to run a business that centers on my love of wood. I have a small but neat woodshop where I come up with ideas and create my art. The work I enjoy most is brainstorming with clients to create custom, one-of-a-kind pieces. As of this writing, the most recent piece was a set of handmade double-six dominos and a custom storage box with a sliding walnut top. This piece was very dear to me, as it would further develop the bond between a daughter and her dad. I am also very excited to say that pieces of my work reside all over the US and Canada, and more recently, internationally.

I truly enjoy working with wood, and I hope your love for the medium will grow as you read this book.

Visit my websites:

Etsy site:
www.etsy.com/shop/mokajadedesigns

Personal site:
www.mokajadewoodstudio.com

Blog:
http://insidemokajade.blogspot.com

introduction

The projects in this book are organized into chapters according to their uses: personal accessories, home décor, wall art, and items for the office. As I mentioned earlier, the subjects of these projects run in several themes. If you would like a cohesive look for your home or office, try making several pieces from one theme.

Circles

This group features the bouyant shape of the circle. The circular motif occurs often in real life, including multi-chromatic soap bubbles floating in the summer air, foam lying on the surface of the ocean, and the shape of the sun, moon, and our very own planet. The circle is also a very modern-looking shape, and these designs would accent a modern, sophisticated home very well.

- **Necklace:** page 26
- **Earrings:** page 32
- **Belt buckle:** page 46
- **Four-square wall art:** page 102
- **File organizer:** page 156
- **Pen holder:** page 142

Cubic

These angular designs evoke the feel of a Japanese shogi, an Etch-a-Sketch, and even memories of geometry class. Try this theme and add some edges and corners to your home's décor.

- **Tissue box cover:** page 166
- **Tea light candle holders:** page 66
- **Photo frame:** page 64

Celtic

I've always been fascinated with the variety of shapes and forms in Celtic designs. Add to that the natural spin that the designs often have, and Celtic quickly became one of my favorite styles. These projects feature motifs that will bring a bit of the Emerald Isle into your home.

- **Earrings:** page 32
- **Keychain:** page 36
- **Tea light candle holders:** page 66
- **Circled wall art:** page 110
- **Framed wall art:** page 130
- **Magnet board:** page 178

Asian

I love the clean lines and spirituality of these Asian designs. Whether you're Buddhist, a fan of koi, or just love the Chinese zodiac, you'll find a project here for your décor.

Insect

Insects are a vital part of our natural world. I especially enjoy the fragile beauty and grace of the butterfly, dragonfly, and bee. If you plant a butterfly garden, watch your backyard pond eagerly for the first dragonfly of the year, or tend a beehive, chances are you'll love these buggy projects!

Botanical

The beautiful curves of a full-blown rose; the rigid lines of bamboo; the graceful and elegant blossoms of the cherry tree and orchid: all of these sophisticated elements can be found within this grouping. It's easy to bring the beauty of these botanical wonders into your home when you create projects from this theme.

getting started

The following chapter serves as a guide to everything that you will need to get started with your scroll sawing hobby. I will guide you through some important safety tips inherent not only to scroll sawing, but to woodworking in general. I focus on the most essential tools and equipment needed, with a few personal suggestions, to make for a successful scrolling experience. To make your projects run smoothly, I also give you a list of the everyday shop essentials you will need. For example: glues, sandpaper, and scroll saw blades—basically anything that is depleted after every project. You will also need measuring and marking tools and some essential hand tools, of which I have provided a complete list. I also provide you with material options, including the difference between using solid wood versus plywood. I also introduce some fun alternative materials, such as plastic acrylic sheets, that can easily be cut on the scroll saw with a few considerations, such as blade choice and scroll saw speed. I also describe the different techniques I employ that work well for me. I am sure you will find the Getting Started chapter a very useful jumping-off point in pursuing your new scrolling hobby. Happy scrolling!

safety tips

Safety is the number one concern when it comes to working in a woodworking shop. When you enter a woodworking shop, a typical woodworker should be wearing: a pair of safety glasses or goggles to protect their eyes; a dust mask or respirator to protect their lungs; and finally, a pair of ear plugs or ear muffs to protect their ears. This is important gear for the safety and health of woodworkers.

DUST PROTECTION

Even though the scroll saw is one of the safest power tools in the workshop, there are a few important safety rules to adhere to. The number one cause for concern when using the scroll saw is the amount of sawdust it generates. It might not have an immediate impact, but over the long term it could cause serious illnesses. To protect against this potential, make sure you have a good dust collection system, including a good air cleaner to get rid of most of the dangerous small sawdust particles from the air. Whether or not you have a system in place, it is a good idea to wear a good particulate dust mask. I wear a disposable NIOSH (National Institute for Occupational Safety and Health)-approved dust mask that has an exhalation valve—a great feature that prevents my safety glasses from fogging up.

EYE PROTECTION

Another important safety concern is the potential for flying wood debris to hit your eyes and face. It is important to wear eye protection at all times in the shop. You will either need prescription safety glasses, which could be quite costly, or some safety over-glasses—a low cost but effective solution. As the name suggests, these could be worn comfortably over your prescription eyeglasses. Your eye protection should also include a face shield when operating machinery such as table saws, lathes, and routers, or any machinery that has a high potential for wood kickback. It will not only protect your eyes, but also your face and neck.

HEARING PROTECTION

Although the scroll saw is not a very noisy machine, when sitting at the scroll saw for long periods of time like I do, noise does become an issue. Wearing a pair of comfortable ear plugs or ear muffs with a good noise reduction rating (NRR) will help prevent gradual hearing loss caused by this prolonged exposure.

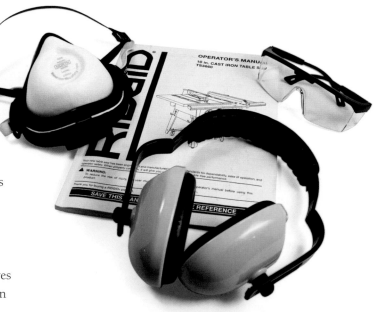

Safety equipment. Before you begin scrolling, be sure to have a dust mask, safety glasses, and ear protection.

FURTHER PROTECTION

In addition to wearing safety gear, you should also be alert when operating the scroll saw. Do not operate the machine when you are fatigued, distracted, or under the influence of any drugs or alcohol. Although the scroll saw will not sever any fingers, it will leave a nasty cut, so always be aware of your hand placement. Also, remove any hanging jewelery, such as bracelets or chains, and get long sleeves and hair out of the way—they can all get caught up in the moving parts of the machine. To help prevent eye strain and injury, make sure you have adequate lighting when operating the scroll saw or any machine in the workshop. Most of all, read all of the owner's manuals for your power tools. Know how to correctly maintain and use your power tools.

Some safety precautions should be considered when you are working with certain finishes. When you are using a spray finish, for instance, always work in a well-ventilated area and wear a respirator equipped with organic vapor cartridges. Always wear protective gloves, especially when working with stains and dyes. I prefer to wear nitrile gloves instead of latex or vinyl; it is more comfortable and offers better protection against volatile substances. It is very durable and will not tear or puncture easily. It is more expensive than latex or vinyl, but in my opinion is well worth the price.

tools and equipment

There are several different tools and pieces of equipment I use in the shop. Some are used more frequently than others, but they all contribute to the completion of a gratifying handmade wooden object. The most used power tools in my shop are the table saw, drill press, and scroll saw. Investing in these three tools will greatly enhance your scrolling projects.

TABLE SAW

With a table saw, you can perform various operations essential to a successful and accurate scroll saw project, especially the ones requiring some sort of joinery. It delivers square corners and edges, and it can cut multiple pieces at the exact same measurement with the aid of the accompanied fence.

I recommend you invest in the best saw you can afford that will fit your needs. There are several styles of table saws.

The portable table saw is great for the casual hobbyist or do-it-yourselfer. It is also used on construction job sites because of its small size and portability. It is the least expensive, but also the least durable.

The contractor saw is a nice midsized table saw that is a favorite of the serious hobbyist and professional furniture and cabinet maker alike. It is less expensive than a cabinet saw, but more rugged than a portable saw. It will offer you the best of both worlds: the portability of the portable saw and the ruggedness of the cabinet saw.

The cabinet saw is a big stationary table saw that requires more room and more power than the other choices. It is also used by the serious hobbyist and professional, and is generally found in production cabinet shops.

DRILL PRESS

Although the drill press is sometimes an undervalued tool, it is an integral part of the scrolling process. It only performs one task, and does it well. It allows you to drill accurate perpendicular holes in wood, metals, and plastics—a must for delicate fretwork.

I have a very basic bench top drill press, although looking back I should have invested a couple more dollars for the extra upgrades—a convenient rack-and-pinion system to easily raise and lower the table, and an attached gooseneck lamp to prevent eyestrain. Since there is a limit to the size of drill bits you can safely use in the drill press, a great addition is a precision pin chuck. This accessory will enable you to safely use small size drill bits in your hefty drill press. Simply fasten the small drill bit in the precision pin chuck, then place this assembly in the chuck of the drill press. You now have a precision machine for your most delicate precision work. Remember to change the spindle speed to the drill bit manufacturer's suggested speed.

SCROLL SAW

Over the years, I have tried a few scroll saws—always the best that I could afford at the time. I am now using a Dewalt with a 20" (508mm) throat depth, an easy-to-use blade tension system, and a conveniently placed variable speed button. It is a robust, smooth-running, quiet machine, and blade change has never been so easy. It requires little maintenance, but I am always sure to blow out or vacuum the sawdust from it after every use. Most saws require regular maintenance, including regular oil lubrications. Some also require part replacements, so whichever saw you purchase, make sure to thoroughly read the owner's manual that comes with the saw. Remember to always release the tension of the blade when the saw is not in use.

OTHER EQUIPMENT

Here is a list of some other tools that will come in handy making the projects in this book. At the beginning of each project, I will provide you with a list of all the tools and materials needed. I will also provide cutting lists.

Power tools
- Router
- Miter saw
- Random orbit sander
- Handheld drill with various size drill bits
- Iron

Measuring and marking tools
- Measuring tape
- Metal ruler
- Combination square
- Set square
- Steel square
- Pencil
- Scratch awl

Hand tools
- Various size clamps
- Chisels
- Mallet
- Ratchet screwdriver
- Utility knife
- Scissors
- Hot glue gun
- Putty knife
- Laminate J-roller
- Glue roller

pendant

TOOLS & MATERIALS

- Drill press
- Drill bits—¹⁄₃₂" (1mm), ³⁄₃₂" (2.5mm) diameter
- Precision pin chuck
- Mini clamps
- Glue gun
- Glue sticks
- Clear packing tape
- Wood glue
- Spray adhesive
- Sandpaper (150–220 grit)
- Pliers
- # 2/0, 2, 5 blades (reverse tooth)
- Leather cord
- Jump ring (optional)
- Stain (optional)
- Finish of choice
- ⅛" (3mm)-thick walnut, sized as desired (big enough to fit the pattern with a bit of room)
- Glue roller

Butterflies are fascinating little creatures. Their brilliantly colored and elegantly shaped wings are truly a work of art many of us try to imitate. In this project, I am trying to capture that beauty in a pendant. The wood I chose for this project is walnut, one of my favorite woods to work with.

The alternate pattern is a design I call Unity 3. I designed this piece to celebrate family and its strength when bonded together. It is a series of connected circles and graceful intertwined curvy lines that loosely represent the human form. The number three represents the number of circles or family members in the design. I cut this pendant from a rich curly maple and finished it with three coats of Danish oil. This would surely make a great gift for your loved one. I will also demonstrate how to tie the adjustable leather cord for the pendant. I will be working with a 36" (914mm) cord length, but you can certainly make the cord whatever length suits your needs.

Butterfly Pendant pattern
Photocopy at 100%

Unity 3 Pendant pattern
Photocopy at 100%

Butterfly Pendant Step-by-Step

1. Attach pattern to prepared stock.
Ensure the top of the stack is slightly sanded so that the pattern can properly adhere to the wood. Use spray adhesive to attach the pattern.

2. Drill the blade entry holes.
A drill press equipped with a precision pin chuck, or a Dremel with a drill press attachment, is recommended to ensure the drill bit is drilled squarely into the wood. Make sure to sand or scrape away any burrs or breakout on the back of the stack.

3. Cut out the pattern starting from the center out.
Thread the blade through a drilled hole, then make all the interior cuts. Because this is a fragile piece, slow down the speed of your scroll saw and keep a steady feed rate.

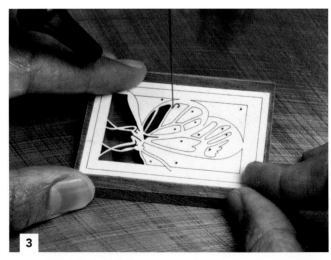

Necklace ideas

I've made many different necklace designs, some of which are shown here. Try scaling down and using a design from another project (Dragon Key Cabinet, page 74; Triple Spiral Earring, page 32). You can also modify an existing pattern—I could have made a Unity pendant with any number of elements. Try backing your pendants with another color of wood to make them pop.

Dragon; Rat; Unity; Triple Swirl; Elements; Horse; Longevity.

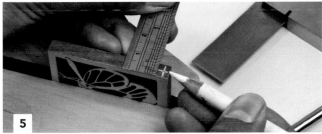

4. Square the edges.
Use a #5 blade to cut the outline shape of the pendant. Use a simple sanding jig (page 189) to sand all edges of the pendant square. It is important that the edges are square to ensure that the cord hole is accurately lined up.

5. Mark the cord hole.
Use a wooden screw clamp to position and clamp the pendant on edge, making sure it is flat on the workbench. If you are using walnut, use a white pencil crayon to mark out the center point on the edge of the pendant. Use a scratch awl to make a small depression on the center point as a guide for the tip of the drill bit.

6. Drill the cord hole.
Carefully drill a ³⁄₃₂" (2.5mm) hole on the center mark. To prevent the drill bit from splitting the underside, drill the hole halfway down from one edge, then flip the piece to complete the hole from the other edge (place another center mark on the other edge). Sand and soften all edges of the pendant to a smooth finish.

7. Tie the adjustable knot in the leather cord.
After the pendant is finished with a clear finish of choice, thread the leather cord through the drilled hole and tie an adjustable knot (see page 30). As an alternative, you can also drill a hole in the face of the pendant and tie the adjustable cord to a jump ring.

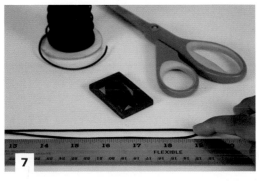

ADJUSTABLE KNOT-TYING TUTORIAL

This process might seem a bit awkward at first, but once you grasp the concept and keep practicing, you will master the art of tying an adjustable knot.

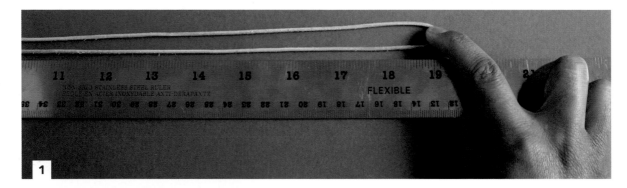

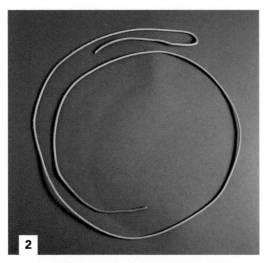

1. Measure the cord.
You will need approximately 28"–36" (711mm–914mm) in cord length. Double up the cord, then measure the length on a ruler or measuring tape to half the final length. Cut with wire cutters or a pair of scissors.

2. Fold one end back.
Remember to thread the pendant onto the cord. If you find that the leather cord is rigid, try dampening it with water. Proceed to fold one end onto itself, making a loop with a tail of about 4" (102mm) in length.

3. Grasp the loop in one hand.
Keep the tail of the loop in the same orientation as seen in Step 2, sandwiched between the top and bottom loops of the cord. Bundle this assembly, with one hand holding the tail and the other hand supporting the loop.

4. Wrap the tail around.
With one hand, grab the tail. Create smaller loops by wrapping the tail around the entire bundle.

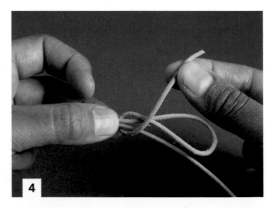

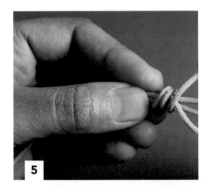

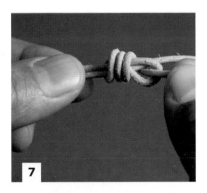

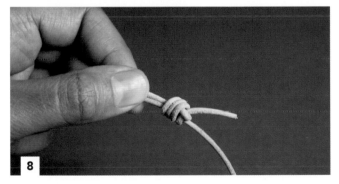

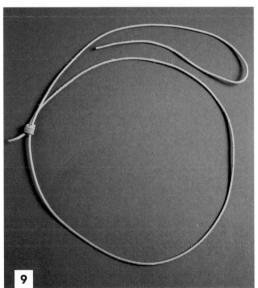

5. Wrap some more.
Continue to wrap the tail around the bundle, making three or more complete loops while still maintaining the original loop on the end of the assembly.

6. Thread the tail.
You should end up with the rest of the tail pointing toward you. Holding the loop assembly securely with one hand, thread the tail end through the original loop.

7. Pull the tail and push the loops.
Grasp the tail end and pull it completely through the original loop. At the same time, push the bundle of the loops until it is taut, but not too tight to prevent the sliding action of the knot.

8. First knot complete.
You should end up with a neat sliding knot made up of three or more complete loops, with the tail end left with enough length for trimming at the end.

9. Tie the second knot.
Repeat Steps 2 to 8 to tie the remaining end.

earrings

TOOLS & MATERIALS

- #1, #5 scroll saw blades
- Drill press
- Mini clamps
- Sand paper (150–220 grit)
- Drill bit, ⅟₁₆" (2mm) diameter
- Spray adhesive
- Clear packing tape
- Oil finish or choice
- Pliers
- Shepherd hooks
- Jump rings (or 24-gauge wire for custom-made jump rings)
- ⅛" or ¼" (3mm or 6mm) walnut or sapele, sized as desired (big enough to fit the pattern with a bit of room)

Wonder what to do with all the little scrap and cut-off hardwood in the shop? The next project is sure to please all of you out there who, like me, cannot bear to part with the littlest piece of perfectly good wood. Earrings are small accessories, but they can make a big impression. I hope my Celtic-inspired pair will make a big impression on you. The symbol I have chosen is the triple spiral, which could have several meanings. The Christian Trinity is the traditional meaning behind this symbol. Another meaning is a representation of earth, water, and sky.

The alternate earring pattern, like the pendant project before, features a design from my Unity series. In this case, however, the design now represents two connected circles or family members. It could personify a mother and child or a couple in love. This time I have chosen to work with sepele wood, which is a type of mahogany. Again, I have finished it with three coats of a rich Danish oil.

On page 41, I will be demonstrating how to make custom jump rings with a rod, some 24-gauge wire, and a pair of wire cutters. The sterling silver shepherd hooks can be found at any jeweler's supply store. You will also need a pair of round-nose pliers, which can be purchased at the same store. I chose to use round-nose pliers because they will not mar your jump rings.

Triple Spiral Earrings pattern
Photocopy at 100%

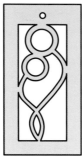

Unity 2 Earrings pattern
Photocopy at 100%

Triple Spiral Earring Step-by-Step

1. Prepare the stock.
Use mini quick clamps to hold the stack in place while you run a bead of hot melt glue on each side of the stack. Drill the blade entry holes.

2. Cut out the pattern.
After you have sanded the back of the stack to get rid of any burrs caused by drilling, use the scroll saw, equipped with a #1 reverse tooth blade, to make all the interior cuts of the pattern.

3

4

5

3. Drill hole for jump ring.
Before cutting out the final shape of the earring, use a drill press equipped with a ⅟₁₆" (2mm) drill bit to drill the hole for the jump ring that will eventually hold the shepherd hook.

4. Cut out the final shape.
After the hole is drilled, it is finally time to cut out the shape of the earring. Use the scroll saw equipped with a #5 reverse tooth blade. Stay as close to the line as possible and sand out any bumps after. Alternately, you can also leave about ⅟₃₂" (1mm) all around and use a drum or edge sander to sand the final shape smooth.

5. Apply a finish to the earrings.
I use a hand-rubbed oil finish on this project to bring out the natural color and enhance the luster of the walnut. Before the finish is applied, be sure to sand the earrings to a smooth finish using the sanding base. Also be sure to soften the edges with 220-grit sandpaper.

6. Attach the findings.
After the finish is completely dry, attach a jump ring and shepherd hook to each earring. Make your own jump rings using 24-gauge wire (see page 41).

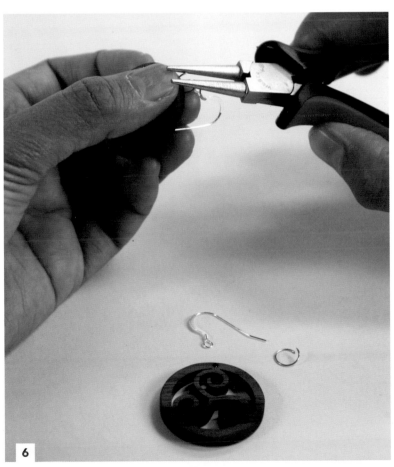

6

keychain

TOOLS & MATERIALS

- Drill press
- Drill bits, 5/64" and 1/16" (1.9mm and 2mm)
- Mini quick clamps
- Glue gun
- Glue sticks
- Spray adhesive
- Sand paper (150–220 grit)
- Scroll saw blades, reverse tooth (# 2/0, 5)
- Wood glue
- Glue roller
- Clear packing tape
- Round-nose pliers
- Wire cutters
- Jump ring
- Key ring
- Round steel rod for making jump rings
- 16-gauge galvanized wire
- Spray finish of choice
- 1/8" (3mm)-thick wood of choice, sized as desired (big enough to fit the pattern with a bit of room)

I have always been fascinated with Eastern cultures and their use of symbolism, including the elements. In Chinese culture, this means earth, water, wood, metal, and fire. I am also intrigued with the easy flow and elegance of brush calligraphy, which is truly inspiring. I wanted to combine these two elements in my keychain design. My contemporary earth element design is wrapped around the traditional Chinese character for "earth." Traditional and contemporary features always make for a stirring combination. The wood I have chosen for this project has nice natural contrasting colors, which is maple for the top and padauk for the backer piece. You can also use stain, dye, or paint to add contrast if you don't have these woods handy.

The alternate pattern is a stunning Celtic-inspired design. It is a stylized form representing the triskelion. It is in the form of three bent legs radiating from the center, giving the appearance of constant motion. This, too, represents different meanings to different cultures, including competition and progress. With this project, I have used two pieces of 1/8" (3mm)-thick Baltic birch plywood. I have stained the backer piece to create a striking contrast. Since I have used a stain, I opted to finish this piece with several coats of a polyurethane spray instead of a hand-rubbed oil finish.

Elements Keychain pattern
Photocopy at 100%

Triskelion Celtic Keychain pattern
Photocopy at 100%

Elements Keychain Step-by-Step

1. Choose the wood.
I like to make the cutout pop by using a contrasting wood for the backer. For this project, I am using maple for the top cutout and padauk for the contrasting backer.

2. Drill blade-entry holes.
After the pattern is temporarily attached to the maple with spray adhesive, use the drill press equipped with the largest drill bit possible; drill the blade entry holes. I am using a 1⁄16" (2mm)-diameter drill bit and drilling the holes as close as possible to a line.

3. Cut the pattern.
Use a #2/0 reverse tooth scroll saw blade to make all interior cuts. Start from the center with the most delicate cuts, moving toward the perimeter and least delicate cuts. Change the blade to #5 to roughly cut around the shape, leaving at least ¹⁄₁₆" (2mm) all around.

4. Glue the top to backer.
After getting rid of the burrs on the back and sanding the inside face of the backer piece, roll an even amount of wood glue to the back of the cutout and clamp it to the backer piece.

5. Drill the jump ring hole.
After the glue is dry, use the drill press equipped with a ⁵⁄₆₄" (1.9mm)-diameter drill bit. Drill a hole at top center. Use a scrap backer piece to avoid tear-out on back.

Elements Keychain Step-by-Step *(continued)*

6. Cut out final shape.
Use a #5 scroll saw blade to cut out the final shape of the keychain. Sand edges to a smooth finish, and soften the sharp corners with 220-grit sandpaper. Protect the keychain with your choice of finish.

7. Assemble the keychain.
To finish off the keychain, simply feed the jump ring through the hole of the piece. Before closing the jump ring, loop the keychain hardware through the jump ring. Finally, crimp the jump ring closed with round-nose pliers.

MAKE CUSTOM JUMP RINGS

You can make many different sizes of jump rings by simply using different rod diameters or anything that is long and uniform in diameter (e.g. screwdriver shafts). All you need is galvanized wire (for this purpose I am using 16 gauge), which can be found at any hardware store, a pair of wire snips, and of course a rod of choice.

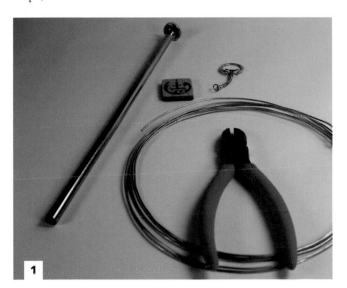

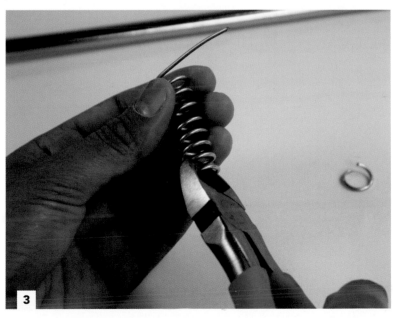

1. Select a rod.
For the size of rod, keep in mind the thickness of material that the jump ring will eventually be looped through. In this case, I am using a ⅜" (10mm)-diameter rod because I will be looping the jump ring through ¼" (6mm)-thick material.

2. Wrap the wire.
Using the 16-gauge wire and gripping one end of the rod, start wrapping the wire around the rod. Make sure the wire is evenly spaced along the rod.

3. Snip the rings.
Remove the wire coil from the rod and snip off each complete loop of the jump ring.

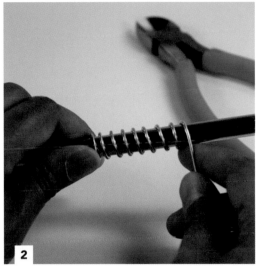

bookmark

TOOLS & MATERIALS

- Drill press
- Glue sticks
- Glue gun
- Spray adhesive
- Sandpaper (150–220 grit)
- Scrap backer material, ⅛" (3mm) plywood
- Spray finish or choice
- Stencil (optional)
- Drill bits, ¹⁄₃₂"–¹⁄₁₆" (1mm–2mm) diameter
- Scroll saw blades, reverse tooth (# 2/0, 5)
- ¹⁄₃₂" (1mm) Finnish birch plywood, sized as desired (big enough to fit the pattern with a bit of room)

The next project is for book lovers and crafters alike. It is, of course, also for those who prefer to give handcrafted gifts with special meaning. My design for the bookmark was inspired by the Chinese zodiac. Instead of looking to the stars for astrological signs, the Chinese zodiac looks to the personalities of animals as birth symbols. I will be concentrating on the Year of the Rat. People born in the Year of the Rat are said to be industrious, shrewd, realistic, inventive, and charming. Does this sound like you? I will also discuss making custom stencils for the optional Chinese character for rat.

The alternate pattern is based on my love of Chinese brush calligraphy. As I mentioned in the keychain project, I love the easy flow and refined elegance of each character. Because this art takes years to master, I can only pay homage to the art the best way I know how, which is through the art of scrolling. If you choose to accompany the scrolled-out character with the English translation, simply make a stencil in the same manner I have illustrated with the rat bookmark.

The wood I will be using is three-ply Finnish birch plywood, also known as aircraft plywood. This is a specialty ply, so you may have to search a bit for the nearest supplier or have it shipped to you. I found my plywood at Lee Valley—a specialty woodworking and gardening store. I prefer this type of ply, because of its strength, flexibility, and nominal thickness—all elements needed for a wooden bookmark. If you weren't born in the Year of the Rat, check out page 197 for the other 11 Chinese zodiac patterns.

MAKE A STENCIL

This step is optional, but it adds a special touch to the bookmark project. You could also use this technique to personalize any of the projects in this book.

Materials needed

- Clear thin plastic (old transparency)
- Pieces of scrap ⅛" (3mm) wood
- Glue gun with hot glue
- Small brush
- Stain or paint of choice

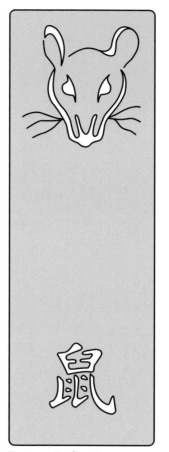

Eastern Zodiac Rat Bookmark pattern

Photocopy at 100%
(See page 197 for the other 11 Chinese zodiac patterns.)

Dream Bookmark pattern

Photocopy at 100%

1. Cut the stencil.

Simply sandwich the plastic material between the two scrap pieces and attach them with a few beads of hot melt glue along the sides. Cut out only the Chinese character, using a #2/0 blade. After the shape of the bookmark is cut out, trace the outline of the rat pattern onto the stencil with a thin felt marker—it helps with alignment later.

2. Stencil the character.

Cut away material on the sides so that you can tape the stencil to the bookmark. Align the stencil. Dip the brush in your choice of stain or paint. Using a paper towel, blot off as much of the finish as possible—too much stain will cause unsightly bleeding under the stencil. In a circular motion, brush on the stain. Carefully remove the stencil to reveal a nice crisp outline of the Chinese character.

Rat Bookmark Step-by-Step

1. Make the stack.
When working with thin material, it is a great idea to stack cut—I suggest five layers. To prevent tearout and give rigidity, use hot glue to attach a piece of ⅛" (3mm) plywood scrap to the bottom. Lightly sand the top of the stack to help the paper pattern fully adhere. There is nothing worse than the pattern lifting up during a cut.

2. Drill blade entry holes.
Use a 1/16" (2mm)-diameter drill bit for the blade entry holes. Make sure to sand away any burrs or tearout left behind from drilling.

3. Cut the pattern.
Use a #2/0 scroll saw blade to complete all interior cuts of the pattern, making sure to work from the center out. Start with the eyes, ears, and, finally, the mouth. Take extra care when veining the whiskers.

4. Cut out the final shape.
After the interior cuts are complete, cut out the final shape of the bookmark by using a #5 reverse tooth blade. Stay as close to the line as possible without removing it completely.

5. Sand and finish.
Do not worry if the line of the outer shape of the bookmark is not straight, as bumps can be sanded out easily by using the flat sanding base. If desired, create and use a stencil for the rat symbol. Line up the bookmarks upside down on a drying rack and spray with clear polyurethane. Allow sufficient drying time. Turn the bookmarks over and spray the fronts.

> **Tip: Double Up Your Patterns**
>
> When it is time to adhere the pattern, consider placing two patterns side-by-side on a wider piece of wood. Not only will this be a great time saver when cutting multiples for gifts or to sell, but also, the wood will be more comfortable to navigate on the scroll saw.

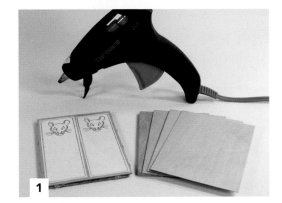

belt buckle

TOOLS & MATERIALS

- Drill press
- Drill bit, 1⁄16" (2mm) diameter
- Scroll saw blades, reverse tooth #2/0, #2, and #5
- Spray adhesive
- White glue
- Glue roller
- Sandpaper (various grits)
- Stain (optional)
- Screws, 3⁄8" (10mm) #4
- Ring and hook buckle back
- Spray finish of choice
- Glue sticks
- Glue gun
- Two pieces of contrasting wood, 1⁄8" (3mm)-thick, sized as desired (big enough to fit the pattern with a bit of room)

How about wearing art around your waist and looking trendy at the same time? The next project will be sure to please. I love this project for its beauty and functionality.

Like butterflies, dragonflies are beautiful and elegant. The dragonfly can mean different things to different cultures. Generally, however, it is a symbol of renewal, change, hope, and love. My design has the dragonfly navigating through reeds of tall grass, destination unknown. The wood I will be using is light-colored ash for the backer piece and a nice contrasting sepele (mahogany) for the top layer.

The alternate pattern is my interlocking circle design. A circle is a fun geometric shape with many meanings and is seen everywhere in nature. With no beginning or end, it can clearly represent infinity and gives us a sense of wholeness and completion. In nature, it can represent the moon, the sun, and more. Interlock a few circles together to create a vibrant moving image. I used a deep brown walnut for the top layer, and a rich contrasting maple for the backer piece. By simply swapping the contrasting layers, you can instantly change the look and feel of the piece.

You will need a snap belt and a ring and hook buckle back. These items can be purchased at any leather supply store. I had a lot of fun making this project and it will surely be a lot of fun to wear. It will also be a great conversation piece.

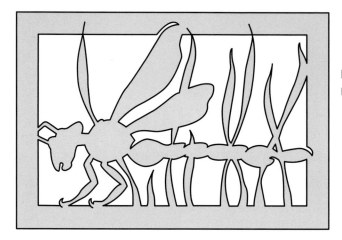

Dragonfly Belt Buckle pattern
Photocopy at 100%.

Circles Belt Buckle pattern
Photocopy at 100%.

Dragonfly Belt Buckle Step-by-Step

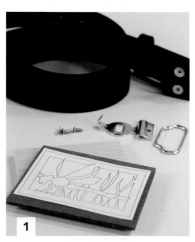

1. Choose the wood for contrast.
Choose combinations of hardwood that offer the best contrast (e.g. poplar and walnut). You can also easily create contrast by staining either the front or back piece of the buckle. For this project, sepele and ash will be used.

2. Attach the scrap backer to the top.
Attach a scrap backer to the top piece to provide rigidity. After applying the pattern, apply clear packing tape to the top before drilling the blade entry holes. This reduces friction and lubricates the blade. Use a glue gun to run several beads of hot melt glue to the sides. Use a mini clamp to keep the stack in place while gluing.

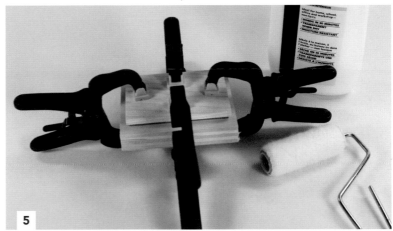

3. Cut the pattern.
Cut out the pattern using a reverse tooth blade. To prevent the delicate parts from snapping off during a cut, place a strip of clear packing tape on them. It is helpful to map out your cutting path before taking a blade to a line.

4. Cut around the outside.
Be sure to leave a bit extra when cutting out the shape of the buckle. I recommend ¹⁄₁₆" (2mm) or so.

5. Glue the top to the back.
Use a glue roller to roll an even layer of white glue on the backside of the cutout. Clamp the sepele top to the ash backer piece using a glue block to ensure even distribution of pressure. Here I am using a scrap piece of ¾" (19mm) thick plywood.

6. Cut out the final shape.
After the glue has dried, cut out the final shape of the buckle on the scroll saw equipped with a #5 reverse tooth blade. To sand the edges smooth, use the edge-sanding jig (see page 189). Soften the sharp edges and corners with 220-grit sandpaper. Apply clear protective finish of choice.

7. Attach hardware.
Locate the ring and hook hardware in the center of the buckle. Using a ¹⁄₁₆" (2mm)-diameter drill bit, drill pilot holes for the screws. Take extra care not to drill too deep, as it would be very unfortunate to drill through to the front. Attach the hardware to the back with ³⁄₈" (10mm) #4 wood screws.

CHAPTER 3
home décor

All of the previous projects have been fun items to adorn or complement the individual. Now I will tackle fun, functional, and fabulous adornments for the home. I will start with smaller and simpler items, such as the coasters that we will make first, and work my way up to larger and more challenging pieces, such as accent lamps. I have designed some functional and great-looking coasters—mix-and-match the demonstration and alternate pattern for a great gift. The next project on the list is a stunning picture frame. What sets this frame apart is the one-of-a kind easel stand. I will also show you my technique for disguising the exposed edges of the plywood we will be using. In the mood for some ambience? How about a glowing tea light holder to set the mood? I will demonstrate a beautiful and modern holder that will fit into any décor. It consists of four squares, and when brought together, it creates one dynamic piece. Are you like me, forever losing your keys? I have a great solution to this very annoying problem—a dedicated key cabinet. Placed by the entrance of your home, it will compel you to always drop your keys off first before you proceed with anything else. The last project in this chapter is a gorgeous accent lamp. It is a bit more difficult than the previous projects, but I will slowly guide you through the process step by step. You will be very proud of yourself for taking on the challenge and finishing this project—and so will I. Whatever the need or occasion, you will find that perfect, rewarding project on the next couple of pages. Keep scrolling!

coasters

TOOLS & MATERIALS

- Drill press
- Precision pin chuck
- Mini clamps
- Drill bit, $\frac{1}{32}$" (1mm)
- Scroll saw blades, reverse tooth #2/0, 5
- Sandpaper (150–220 grit)
- Spray adhesive
- Polyurethane glue
- Spray finish or choice (interior/ exterior spray varnish)
- Stain (optional)
- Clear, small, non-slip pads
- Cork backing
- Utility knife
- Alder
- Walnut

The square shape of the coaster is simple, yet elegant, with a delicately cut bee design. I have included a dragonfly design as an alternate pattern. You can make a single set of bees, or you can mix-and-match the set with dragonflies.

The wood I will be using is alder for the top layer and a contrasting walnut for the bottom layer. Since the coasters will be used in the presence of moisture, special attention should be paid to the kind of adhesive and protective finish that will be used. I prefer to use a polyurethane adhesive and more than three coats of a spray finish. Ensure that the finish coats the inside edges of the cutouts. Presented in a box, a coaster set makes a perfect gift.

CUTTING LIST

Part #	Amount	Part Name	Measurement	Material
1	4	Top	3 ¾" x 3 ¾" x ⅛" (95mm x 95mm x 3mm)	Alder
2	4	Bottom	3 ¾" x 3 ¾" x ¼" (95mm x 95mm x 6mm)	Walnut

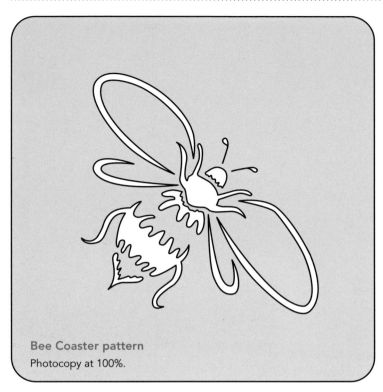

Bee Coaster pattern
Photocopy at 100%.

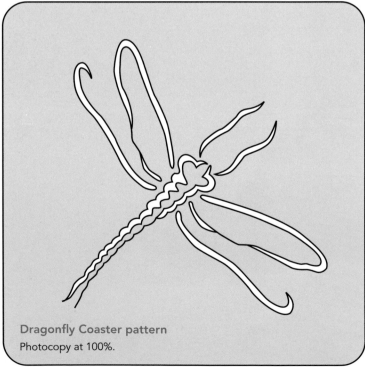

Dragonfly Coaster pattern
Photocopy at 100%.

Bee Coaster Step-by-Step

1. Choose the wood.
For this project, I have chosen walnut for contrasting backing and alder for the top. Alder is a great renewable wood source since it grows fast and furious. Clamp the stack of two tops using mini clamps. Use the hot glue gun to apply strips of glue approximately 1" (25mm) apart on all four sides.

2. Cut out the pattern.
Use a precision pin chick and a ½2" (1mm) drill bit to drill blade entry holes. Use a #2/0 reverse tooth blade to cut out the pattern. Attach clear packing tape to hold the delicate parts in place. Use a #5 reverse tooth blade to cut out the rough shape of the coaster.

3. Trace the outer edge of the coaster.
The outline of the coaster on the second top is gone after you cut the stack to rough shape. I use a clear plastic template to redraw the outline shape. Obtain a transparency or any clear scrap plastic. Draw the final outline of the coaster with a fine tip felt pen and cut out the plastic template with a utility knife.

4. Glue the top to walnut backer.
Sand the burrs from the back of the top cutout. Polyurethane glue requires the addition of moisture to cure. Spread an even, very thin layer of glue to the top of the walnut backer. Moisten the back of the alder top with water. Use a glue block to clamp the pieces for at least 4 hours.

> **Tip: Stain Option**
>
> If you want to stain part of the coaster instead of using different woods, make sure you stain the wood first. Wait for it to dry before you continue with your project.

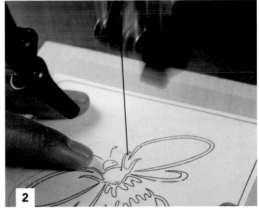

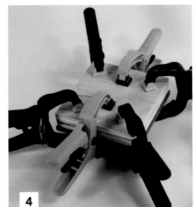

5. Cut out the final shape.

Use a #5 reverse tooth blade to cut out the final shape of the coaster. Cut just on the outer edge of the line. Another option is to cut approximately ½₂" to ⅛₆" (1mm to 2mm) around and use a sanding drum attached to a drill press, or an edge sander, to sand to the final shape and outline of the coaster.

6. Clean up edges and finish.

To clean up the edges of the coaster, use the edge-sanding jig (page 189). Sand the entire coaster to a smooth finish using 150–220 grit sandpaper. Soften the sharp corners and edges of the coaster. Finally, apply three or more coats of a water-resistant spray finish. Apply a nonslip clear pad in each corner of the back of the coaster. Alternately, you can apply a cork backer to the back of the coaster.

picture frame

TOOLS & MATERIALS

- Table saw
- Router
- Rabbeting router bit, ¼" (6mm) diameter
- Drill press
- Disc sander (or files and sandpaper)
- Clamps
- Drill bits, 5⁄64" and 1⁄16" (1.9mm and 2mm)
- Hand drill
- Scroll saw blades, reverse tooth #2 and 5
- Clear packing tape
- Scrap backer material
- Sandpaper
- Double-sided tape
- Glass, 4"x 6"x ⅛" (102mm x 152mm x 3mm)
- Turns
- Finishing nail/brass rod
- Toothpick
- Manual screwdriver
- Brass screws, #4
- Spray finish
- Wood glue
- White glue
- Glue roller
- Wooden screw clamp
- Sepele and Baltic birch (or maple)
- ¼" (6mm)-thick mahogany plywood
- Shallow container
- Stain or dye of choice

A picture frame is a great way to showcase the people that you love, family and friends alike. What makes this picture frame extra-special is that it was handcrafted by you. The frame is completely crafted by hand, right down to the custom easel stand. You will need some picture frame turn buttons, purchased at any framing store, and a custom-cut piece of 4"x 6" (102mm x 152mm) glass. I purchased my glass at a windshield repair business. I will also discuss how to veneer the edges of exposed plywood, since I will be using Baltic birch ply for this project. Of course, if you choose to use solid wood, this step is not necessary. I hope you enjoy making this project as much as I have.

My design for the picture frame came from my love of the beautiful and delicate orchid. I also wanted to offset the delicate curving lines of the orchid with the straight and rigid lines of the *shoji*-like framework on the left. (*Shoji* are Japanese paper screens with wooden support framing.) Even though I brought two very different elements together, I think they work together nicely.

CUTTING LIST

Part #	Amount	Part Name	Measurement	Material
1	1	Top	⅛" x 7 1⁄16" x 9" (3mm x 179mm x 229mm)	Baltic birch
2	1	Backer	⅝" x 7 1⁄16" x 9" (16mm x 179mm x 229mm)	Baltic birch
3	1	Back insert	¼" x 4" x 6" (6mm x 102mm x 152mm)	Mahogany plywood
4	1	Stand blank	⅜" x 2" x 6" (10mm x 51mm x 152mm)	Baltic birch
5	1	Glass insert	⅛" x 4" x 6" (3mm x 102mm x 152mm)	Glass

Orchid Picture Frame pattern
Make 1 copy at 120%

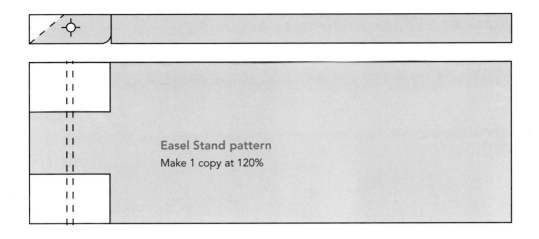

Easel Stand pattern
Make 1 copy at 120%

Orchid Picture Frame Step-by-Step

1. Choose and prepare stock.
Cut all parts on a table saw equipped with a combination blade.
Use the cutting list to cut all pieces to size. Number all parts to
prevent confusion.

2. Cut out the pattern.
If you choose to make multiple frames at the same time, stacking
multiple tops is a great time-saver. Use masking tape to keep parts
together. Apply the paper pattern with spray adhesive and drill
blade-entry holes with a ⅟₁₆" (2mm) bit. Cut out the orchid with a
#2 reverse-tooth blade. Switch to a #5 reverse tooth blade for the
rectangular shapes. Leave the window for later.

1

2

Orchid Picture Frame Step-by-Step *(continued)*

3. Attach the backer.
Use the simple right-angle alignment jig (page 192) to temporarily attach the top to the backer with a few strips of double-sided tape. To ensure that the parts stay together firmly, apply light clamp pressure wherever the tape is applied.

4. Cut out the window opening.
Use a scroll saw with a #5 reverse tooth blade to cut out the window opening. This leaves an exact opening in both the top and backer.

5. Rout out the rabbet on rear of the picture frame.
The rabbet on the back of the frame is best done with a router table equipped with a ¼" (6mm) rabbetting bit. The ¼" x ⅜" (6mm x 10mm) rabbet will house the glass and back insert. Feed the picture frame counter-clockwise. Make a couple of passes by raising the bit ⅛" (3mm) at a time to reduce strain on the bit.

6. Square the corners of the rabbets.
You will notice that the router bit leaves the corners rounded. An easy fix is to use a 1" (25mm) chisel to square the corners. As an alternative to squaring the corners, you could instead round the corners of the back insert to match the rounded corners left by the router.

7. Make the easel back stand.
A pivot pin is needed (e.g. brass rod or finishing nail with head and tip snipped off). Use spray adhesive to glue the pattern to the stand blank. With the blank trapped in a wooden screw clamp, drill the hole on the edge. For a finishing nail, use a ⁵⁄₆₄" (1.9mm) bit. Locate the hole at center. Drill only just beyond the line marking part B.

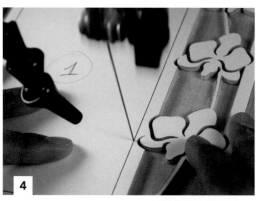

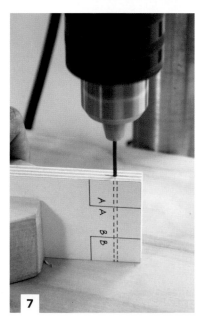

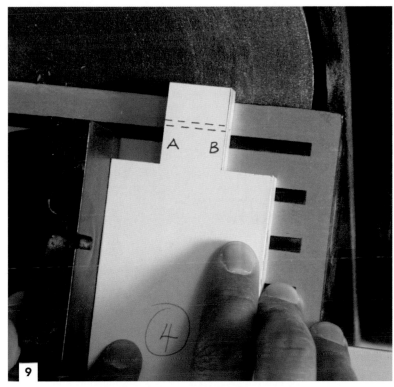

8

9

8. Cut corners.
After the pivot pin hole is drilled, use a scroll saw with a #5 reverse tooth blade to cut off the top corners of the stand blank. Don't throw them away—they'll hold the pivot pin in place. Be sure to number or mark the cutoffs accordingly.

9. Shape and bevel the stand blank.
Use a disc sander with the table tilted at 45˚ to bevel the center part of the stand. The same effect can be achieved with files and sandpaper. Round the bottom of the 45˚ angle to prevent the center from binding. Keep the top crisp and square.

10. Shape the cutoffs.
To ensure proper function of the easel stand pivot, the lower front edges of the cutoffs will also need sanding. Do this by rounding the cutoffs on the sanding bases.

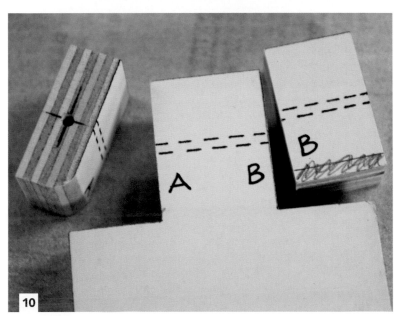

10

Orchid Picture Frame Step-by-Step *(continued)*

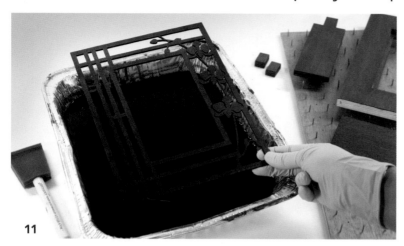

11. Apply a stain.
After separating the top from the backer using a large paint scraper and a gentle side-to-side motion, mark which way is up. Sand all parts, including the easel stand, to a smooth finish. Pour some stain or dye into a shallow container then dip the cutout into it and brush all other parts, remembering to leave the top of the backer for contrast (surface that shows through the cutout).

12. Glue top to backer.
After the stain or dye is dry, glue the top to the backer. Use the right-angle alignment jig (page 192). Roll an even layer of white glue to the underside of the top, and then carefully lay the top onto the backer, which is already seated in the jig. Apply clamps.

13. Sand and veneer.
After the glue is dry, clean up the edges of the frame with a sanding block. Veneer all exposed plywood edges to finish off the frame nicely.

14. Glue the stand parts to the back insert.
Measure in 1¼" (32mm) from the top and 1" (25mm) from the sides. Mark these measurements with low-tack masking tape. Mark the part letters on the back of the stand parts. Temporarily insert the pivot pin. Brush glue on the cutoffs of the stand only. Place in position and carefully clamp in place.

15. Apply a finish.

After the glue is dry on the easel back assembly, remove the long pivot pin to free center part of stand. Place all parts on a drying rack and spray on several coats of finish. Allow to dry, and lightly sand between each coat with fine-grit sandpaper.

16. Insert pivot pin.

After the parts of the easel stand are dry, insert the pivot pin, making sure it goes through all the parts. Glue a section of toothpick to plug the hole left behind. Carefully trim the toothpick flush using a chisel. Dab some stain on the end of the exposed toothpick.

17. Attach the turns.

Assemble the picture frame by inserting the glass, your photo, and the easel stand assembly. Use a ¹⁄₁₆" (2mm) drill bit to drill one pilot hole on each side of the frame for the turns. Finally, screw in the #4 brass screws using a manual screwdriver.

15

16

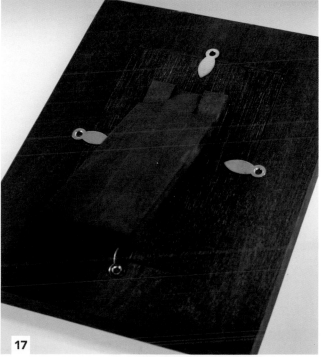

17

cubic picture frame

The alternate picture frame design is a very symmetrical and geometric design that I call Cubic. I enjoy playing around with geometric shapes to create very graphic and dynamic designs. I then like to further enhance my design by using contrasting woods or by simply coloring some part of the piece with dye or stain. Again, I use veneer to disguise the exposed plywood edges and then simply stain it to finish it.

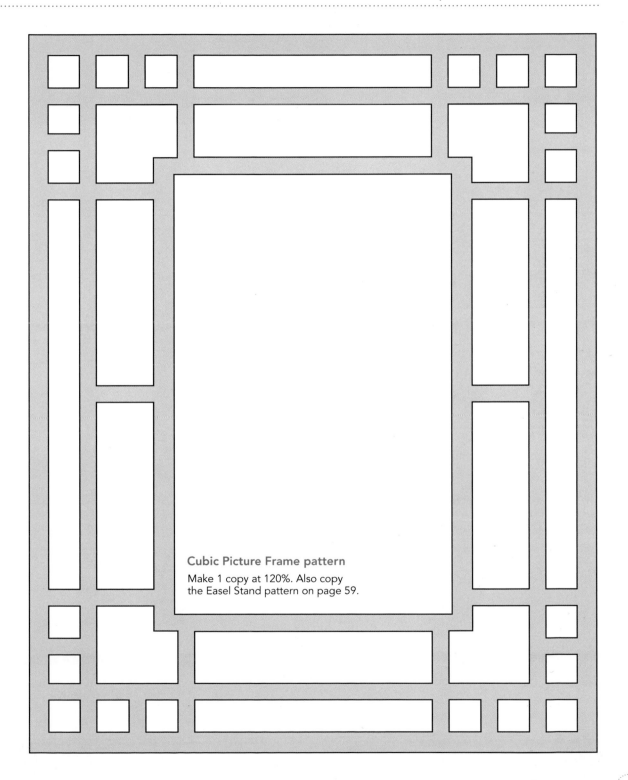

Cubic Picture Frame pattern

Make 1 copy at 120%. Also copy
the Easel Stand pattern on page 59.

square tea light holder

TOOLS & MATERIALS

- Table saw
- Drill press
- Miter saw
- Drill bit, 1/16" (2mm)-diameter brad point
- Forstner bit, 1⅝" (41mm)
- Scratch awl
- Glue gun
- Glue sticks
- Spray adhesive
- Wood glue
- Glue roller
- Band clamps
- Spray finish
- Sandpaper (various grits)
- Putty knife
- Stain (optional)
- Shallow container
- Scroll saw blades, reverse tooth #5
- Double-sided tape
- Maple plywood, ¾" (19mm)
- Baltic birch, ⅛" (3mm), ¼" (6mm)

There is nothing more soothing, spiritual, and sensual than a burning candle. It can be a comfort after a long hard day, a light in a moment of darkness, or a warm romantic glow at a dinner for two. A well-made handcrafted holder elevates the appeal of a burning candle.

My design for this candle holder has a geometric, modern feeling, which I call my Cubic series. I love how intersecting straight lines can create such a bold and graphic aesthetic, especially when you use two contrasting colors as illustrated here. The intersecting lines also help to bring the four holders together to create one dynamic design.

The construction of the holders is simple and straightforward. The specialty tool you will need for this project is the 1⅝" (41mm) diameter Forstner bit or saw tooth bit, to drill the opening necessary to house the candle. Please take note of a few safety issues associated with a wooden candle holder. Never place the candle directly in the opening; always use the metal housing that comes with the tea light candle. Never leave a burning candle unattended. Here's to a glowing project!

CUTTING LIST

Part #	Amount	Part Name	Measurement	Material
1	4	Top	⅛" x 4½" x 4½" (3mm x 114mm x 114mm)	Baltic birch
2	4	Base core	¾" x 4" x 4" (19mm x 102mm x 102mm)	Maple ply
3	16	Edging strips	¼" x 1¼" x 4½" (6mm x 32mm x 114mm)	Baltic birch

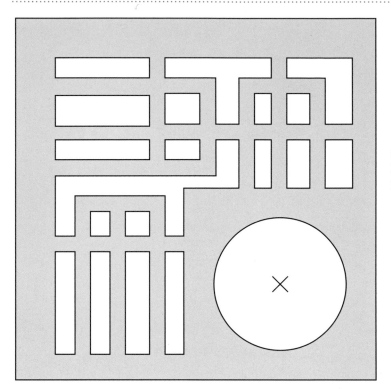

Cubic Square Tea Light Holder pattern
Make 1 copy at 125%

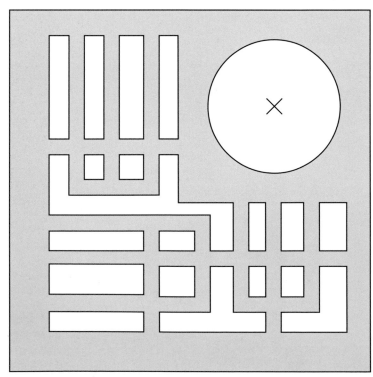

Cubic Square Tea Light Holder Step-by-Step

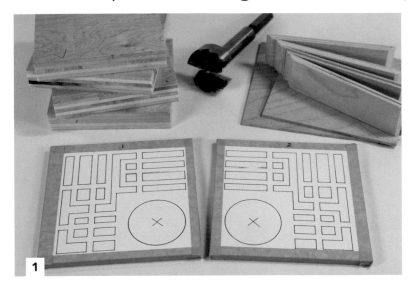

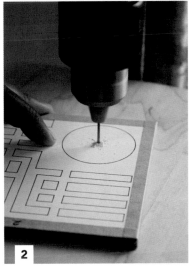

1. Choose the wood and prepare parts.

Cut all parts on a table saw equipped with a plywood or crosscut blade. Leave the edging strip fairly long so it can be mitered to final length on the miter saw at a later stage. I left it long enough so I can get at least 8 edging pieces from one edging strip. Since we need 16 pieces, I made two long edging strips. Stack 2 tops together with a pattern and apply masking tape to the edges. You should have 2 stacks with 2 tops each, 1 stack each for the right and left sides of the tea light holder.

2. Drill blade entry holes.

Use a drill press with a ¹⁄₁₆" (2mm)-diameter brad point bit to drill all blade entry holes, including a pilot hole to register the position of the 1⅝" (41mm) Forstner bit. Use a scratch awl to start the pilot hole. This ensures the tip of the bit will accurately engage and drill the hole in the right position.

3. Cut the pattern.

Use a #5 reverse tooth scroll saw blade to cut out the pattern, making sure to work from the center toward the outside. Scrolling inside corners is difficult. Leave the corners rounded and then go in afterwards to square up the rounded corners.

4. Cut miters into edging.

Use a miter saw or a miter box and a handsaw to cut 45° miters onto the edging. To get all 16 pieces of edging to the same length, clamp a stop block to the miter saw. Before you clamp the stop block to the miter saw, make sure to cut a miter on one end of the edging strip first. Measure and mark the length of the first edging piece, clamp the stop block accordingly, and then cut the first edging piece to length. Now all you have to do is flip the edging strip over from back to front to cut the second piece to length. Continue in this manner to get all 16 edging pieces cut to the exact same length, making sure to flip the strip after each cut.

Cubic Square Tea Light Holder Step-by-Step *(continued)*

5. Attach the edging.
Spread wood glue on the edges of the base and miters of the edging; clamp together using a band clamp.

6. Temporarily attach top to base.
Sand the top of the base assembly to flush up the edging to the base. Use double-sided tape to temporarily attach the top to the base.

7. Set the depth of the candle hole.
Simply draw a depth line ⅝" (16mm) down from the top of the assembly. Mount the Forstner bit in the drill press and lock in the depth at the drawn depth line.

8. Drill the candle hole.
Use the 1⁄16" (2mm) pilot hole drilled earlier to locate and drill a hole using the 1⅝" (41mm) Forstner bit. Slow down the drill press spindle speed to 500 rpm for soft woods and 200 rpm for hard woods. Make several shallow plunges and get rid of shavings between each plunge. This will prevent the drill bit from getting bogged down and overheating.

Tip: Effective Miter Clamp

The best clamp for miters is a roll of clear packing tape. Not only does the tape bring the miters together for a snug fit, but also, you have visibility through the clear tape to verify the fit.

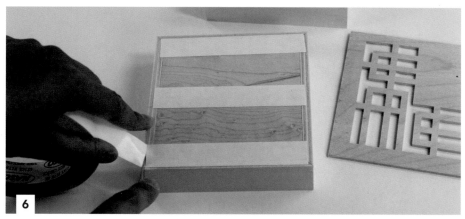

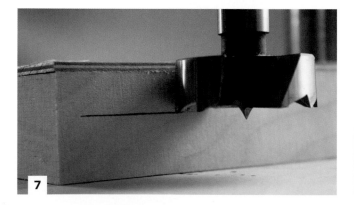

9. Sand all parts.
Make sure to sand the sides of the top flush to the box with a sanding block. I am using a wooden hand screw clamp as a vice. Lay out the various grits of sandpaper for easy accessibility.

10. Separate the tops.
Carefully separate the tops from the base assemblies by using a wide putty knife or paint scraper. Be sure to mark and match each top to each base assembly. Remove all residues left from the double-sided tape by using nail polish remover, mineral spirits, or acetone.

11. Stain all parts before assembly.
Sand the tops of the base assemblies and remove any burrs from the back of the cutouts. Pour some stain or dye of choice in a shallow container and dip the cutouts into the mixture. Stain all parts of the holder except for the top of the box base. Use a foam brush to stain the candle hole recess.

12. Assemble and finish.
Use a glue roller to carefully spread wood glue on the back of the cutouts and clamp them to their corresponding bases. Align each one carefully and use glue blocks to evenly distribute the clamp pressure. Apply a coat of a clear spray finish to the holder. Allow the finish to dry, lightly sand with fine grit sandpaper, and apply another coat. Repeat for up to 3 to 4 coats of finish.

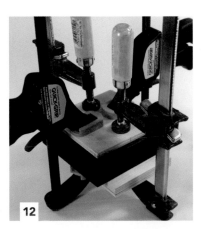

celtic shield knot square tea light holder

The alternate tea light holder design is loosely based on a Celtic shield knot. It is a symbol of protection that adorned the shields of ancient warriors. I chose this design because it lends itself nicely to the four individual shapes of the holder. Individually, each shape can hold its own, but bring the four squares together to reveal a more dynamic and much stronger design. Not unlike the strength of a shield knot—which has no beginning and no end.

**Celtic Square Tea
Light Holder pattern**
Make 1 copy at 125%

key cabinet

TOOLS & MATERIALS

- Table saw
- Dado blade
- Router
- Router table
- Straight router bit
- Drill press
- Brad point bit, ⁵⁄₃₂" (4mm)
- Hand drill
- Countersink
- Scroll saw blades, reverse tooth #2 and #5
- Random orbit sander
- Right-angle alignment jig (page 192)
- Edge sanding jig (page 189)
- Clamps
- Glue gun
- Glue sticks
- Wood glue
- Spray adhesive
- Rotary tool, such as Dremel
- Right angle attachment for rotary tool
- Small ratchet screwdriver
- 2 no-mortise hinges
- 1 knob (includes screw)
- 1 door catch
- 6 ¾" (19mm)-deep square hooks
- Wood screws, #6 ½" (13mm), 2 (top)
- Wood screws, #4 ⅜" (10mm), 12 (8 for hinges, 4 for catch)
- Veneer tape
- Iron
- Sandpaper (various grits)
- Brad nails, ½" (13mm)
- Stain of choice
- Veneer dots
- Brass washers and appropriate screws for hanging cabinet on wall

Are you always losing your keys? I have a great solution in the form of a dedicated key cabinet, which will not only help you to keep track of your keys, but also be an eye-pleasing addition to the front entrance of your home.

The design of the box itself is simple, with clean lines and a Shaker-style door that frames the exquisite dragon design. The dragon symbolizes courage and strength, and is also a protector of treasures—in this case, your keys. The wood I will be using is Baltic birch plywood with a veneered edge. From now on, you will always know where your keys are!

CUTTING LIST

Part #	Amount	Part Name	Measurement	Material
1	2	Sides	⅜" x 2½" x 9¼" (10mm x 64mm x 235mm)	Baltic birch
2	1	Sub-top	⅜" x 2½" x 7" (10mm x 64mm x 178mm)	Baltic birch
3	1	Bottom	⅜" x 2½" x 7" (10mm x 64mm x 178mm)	Baltic birch
4	1	Back	¼" x 7" x 9" (6mm x 178mm x 229mm)	Baltic birch
5	1	Top	⅜" x 3" x 8¼" (10mm x 76mm x 210mm)	Baltic birch
6	2	Hook rails	¼" x 6½" x 1" (6mm x 165mm x 25mm)	Baltic birch
7	1	Door base	¼" x 6⅜" x 8⅜" (6mm x 162mm x 213mm)	Mahogany plywood
8	2	Door rails	⅜" x 1" x 4¼" (10mm x 25mm x 108mm)	Baltic birch
9	2	Door stiles	⅜" x 1" x 8⅜" (10mm x 25mm x 213mm)	Baltic birch
10	1	Door panel	⅛" x 4¼" x 6⅜" (3mm x 108mm x 162mm)	Baltic birch

Dragon Key Cabinet pattern
Make 1 copy at 115%

Dragon Key Cabinet Step-by-Step

1. Prepare the stock.
With the cutting list handy, cut all parts on the table saw. Leave some extra length on the hook rails so they can be cut to fit at a later stage. Always number each part according to the cutting list. This project requires a lot of hardware, so be sure to account for all pieces.

2. Prepare case parts for rabbets.
To keep track of where each rabbet will be cut, lay out the appropriate parts and mark each corresponding end. Determine the back edges of each part. Next, mark the width and depth of the rabbets on all parts.

3. Cut rabbets on sides to receive sub-top and bottom.
Use the table saw, equipped with a ⅜" (10mm) stacked dado blade, to cut a ¼" (6mm)-wide by ⅜" (10mm)-deep rabbet on each end of each side. If you have a router table, a straight bit can be used to achieve the same result. Because we are rabbetting the ends of the sides, we will have to use the table saw miter gauge to guide the piece over the dado blade. And because we need to ensure that the rabbet is in the same location on each end, we will need to clamp a stop block to the miter gauge. To be able to do this, we need to attach a board to the miter gauge to act as a sacrificial or auxiliary fence. The fence will be long enough so that we can clamp a stop block to it and it will also back up the side piece, which will prevent tear out on the back edge. Be sure to set the height of the dado blade first.

4. Cut the remaining rabbets to receive the back.
Cut the rabbets ¼" (6mm) deep by ¼" (6mm) wide on the back edges of each side, sub-top, and bottom to receive the ¼" (6mm)-thick back. Run the pieces along the table saw fence over the dado blade. Since it is more convenient to keep the ⅜" (10mm)-wide dado setup, it is important to equip your commercial fence with a wooden auxiliary fence (see sidebar).

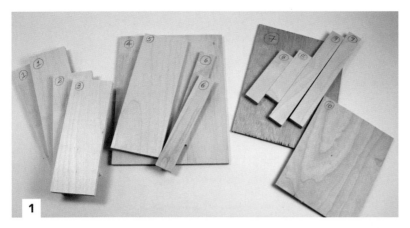

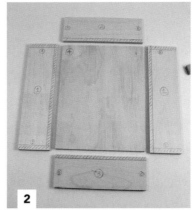

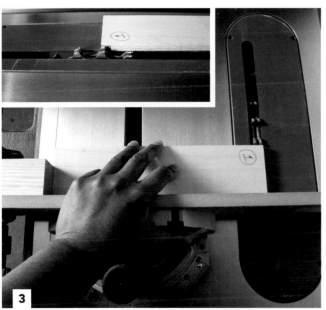

5. Pre-sand case parts.
After all the rabbets are cut, use a random orbit sander to sand all interior surfaces of case parts to a smooth finish. It is easier to sand the interior surfaces before assembly. If you have opted to stain the cabinet, now is a good time to stain the interior surfaces as well.

6. Build the case.
Dry fit the parts before gluing. If you are happy with the fit, glue the sub-top and bottom into the end rabbets of one side. Then glue and slide the other side into place.

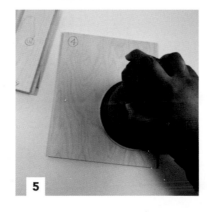

Dragon Key Cabinet Step-by-Step *(continued)*

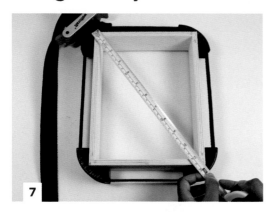

7. Clamp the case.
Use a band clamp or clear packing tape to clamp in place. Finally, ensure that the case is square by measuring on the diagonals.

8. Attach the back.
Once the case assembly is square, run a bead of glue in the corner of the rabbets and insert the back. Nail in place with brads. Always keep in mind the amount of rabbet surface you have to nail into.

9. Veneer edges of case (optional).
Align the inside edges of the veneer to the inside edges of the case. Use the iron to attach the veneer to the top and bottom edges of the case first, then the sides. Do not glue down the veneer on the corners. The side veneers will overlap the top and bottom veneers.

10. Veneer the corners of case (optional).
Use a sharp utility knife to cut tight-fitting butt joints. Utilize the side veneer as a guide, and trim the top and bottom veneers. Iron down the corners. Trim the excess veneer along the outer edge of the case with a sharp utility knife. Use a file to clean the inside edges of the veneer. Also remember to veneer the exposed edges of the top piece. Sand the outside of the case and the top piece to a smooth finish.

Making a wooden auxiliary fence

Equipping your table saw with a wooden sacrificial fence will help you avoid any safety issues or ruining your perfectly good commercial fence.

1. Simply attach a scrap piece of wood to your fence.
2. Lower the dado blade down so it is well below the table surface.
3. Slide the fence over the blade approximately the width of the rabbet.
4. Turn on the saw; slowly and carefully raise the blade to approximately the height of the rabbet. The dado blade will now be buried under the auxiliary fence.

Wood auxiliary fences will protect your original fence.

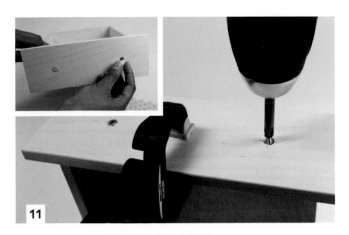

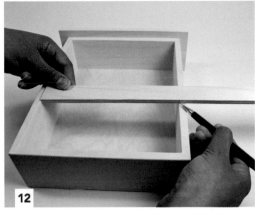

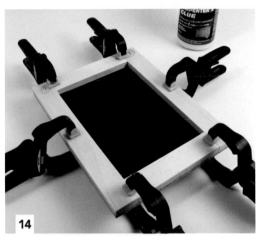

11. Attach the top.
Position the top on the case. The ends of the top should overhang the sides evenly. The back edge of the top should be flush to the back of the cabinet. Clamp the top in place and drill two holes with a countersink bit. Attach the top with #6½" (13mm)-long wood screws. To conceal the screw holes, use adhesive-backed veneer dots (I found mine at Lee Valley).

12. Measure and cut the hook rails.
Determine the length of the hook rails by holding the hook rail parts on the inside edge of the cabinet and marking the inside of the other end. This method ensures a perfect fit. Cut to length.

13. Glue the hook rails in place.
Before gluing the hook rails in place, use the drill press to drill holes to receive the hooks. With the aid of a 3" (76mm) spacer block and a deep glue block, glue into position and clamp the hook rails in place.

14. Build the door.
Pre-stain the top of the door base (#7). After the stain is dry, use the right-angle alignment jig (page 192) to glue the rails and stiles to the door base. Clamp in place, making sure to place a clamp on the butt joints.

15. Cut out the pattern.
While the door assembly is drying, cut out the pattern. Use a hot glue gun to attach the door panel to a scrap backer. Use a ¹⁄₁₆" (2mm) drill bit in the drill press for the scroll saw blade entry holes. Use a #2 or #5 reverse tooth blade to cut out the pattern.

Dragon Key Cabinet Step-by-Step *(continued)*

16. Veneer edges of door assembly.
Clean up all glue squeeze-out. Cut a piece of ¾" (19mm)-wide veneer tape longer than the intended edge. Place the veneer on the edge and slowly move a hot iron from one end to the other. Next, use a J-roller or a block of wood to burnish the veneer. I prefer to start with the top and bottom of the door, flush the edges and ends of the strip, and then veneer the sides.

17. Cut the door panel to size.
Determine the exact size of the door panel by measuring the inside edge of the door recess. Draw a new outline on the pattern to adjust the size accordingly. Use the scroll saw with a #5 reverse tooth blade to cut the door panel to size. Clean up the edges of the door panel with the use of the edge-sanding jig (page 189).

18. Glue the door panel to the door recess.
Roll an even layer of white glue onto the back of the door panel. Drop the door panel into the door recess. Place a glue block the size of the door opening onto the door panel and clamp in place.

19. Attach the hinges.
I prefer to attach hinges to the cabinet first. To drill the screw holes, I suggest the use of a right angle attachment on a rotary tool. Attach a piece of masking tape on the drill bit as a flag to indicate the depth of the hole. This will prevent you from drilling out through the other side of the cabinet side.

20. Position the door in the opening.
Position the door in the opening of the cabinet by using veneer pieces as shims to get even spacing all the way around. An ideal space opening size around the door is approximately 1/16" (2mm) or the thickness of a dime. Mark the hinge position on the door and drill screw holes. Fasten the door in place.

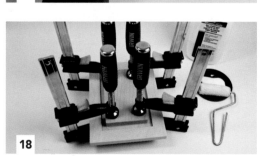

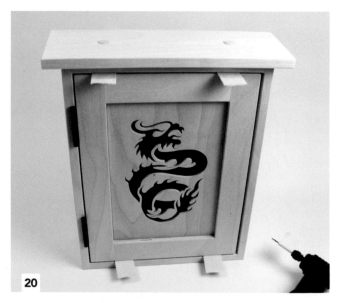

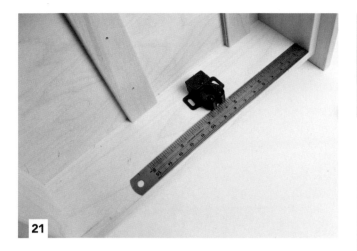

21

21. Attach the door catch.
Attach the bigger part of the catch a little more than halfway up on the inside of the cabinet. Screw the part in place using the ratchet screwdriver.

22. Attach the smaller part of the catch.
Clip the smaller part of the catch into position in the bigger part of the catch. Close the door and gently press. Since the back of the catch has little teeth, this action will leave little locator indentations for easy alignment. Find the indentation, position the part, and screw in place.

23. Attach the doorknob.
I like to place the doorknob approximately halfway on the cabinet door. Not only is this pleasing to the eye, but it also prevents the door from racking when it is opened. Use a 5⁄32" (4mm)-diameter brad point bit to drill the hole to receive the screw. Place a backer block to the back of the door to prevent tear out.

24. Attach the key hooks.
Use round-nose pliers to install a hook 1¼" (32mm) from both ends of the hook rails. Center the third hook. Drill two screw holes through the back to hang the cabinet to the wall. Use brass washers and appropriate screws to hang the cabinet to the wall. Make sure to also use appropriate anchors for your wall to secure the cabinet.

22

23

24

bamboo key cabinet

The alternate design for the key cabinet is the bamboo design. It differs slightly from the demo design, not in construction, but in the subject of design as well as color. Bamboo is a symbol of good fortune in many Asian cultures. Bamboo is used in the practice of Feng Shui, which brings the five elements of water, fire, earth, wood, and metal together to create a more balanced home life. Because of its strength, bamboo is used in the home to enhance the positive flow of energy. Because the color red is also considered a color of good luck in Asian culture, I chose to stain the key cabinet a rich red mahogany tone to further enhance this symbolism. As I mentioned in the demo, if you choose to stain your cabinet, it is a good idea to pre-stain the inside of the case parts before it is glued and assembled. The door is also treated differently. Instead of staining the top of the door base, stain the rails and stiles of the door first and then glue these parts to the door base. After the glue is dry, veneer the edges of the door and then proceed to stain the rest of the door. After the pattern is cut out on the door panel, stain it as well.

Bamboo Key Cabinet pattern
Make 1 copy at 110%

accent lamp

TOOLS & MATERIALS

- Table saw
- Miter saw
- Router and router table
- Router straight bit, ¼" (6mm) diameter
- Drill press
- Drill bit, ⅟₁₆" (2mm) diameter
- Brad point bit, ²⁵⁄₆₄" (10mm) diameter
- Scroll saw blades, reverse tooth #2 and 5
- Band clamps, 3
- Chisels
- Mallet
- Wood glue
- Glue sticks
- Glue gun
- Spray adhesive
- Sandpaper (various, including 320 grit)
- Acrylic adhesive
- Low-wattage chandelier bulb
- Lighting acrylic
- Miter box/back saw
- ¾" (19mm)-diameter dowel x ⁵⁄₁₆" (8mm) long
- Utility knife
- Putty knife
- Clear packing tape
- Steel square
- Stain (optional)
- Spray finish of choice
- Electrical cord with plug and in-line switch
- Candelabra socket
- 1¼" (32mm) threaded nipple
- Nut and washer
- Cardboard sleeve (comes with the short hickey)
- Wire strippers
- Screwdriver (Phillips or flathead bit)

An accent lamp is a great way to add ambience to any room where too much or too little light is not acceptable. This project is a little more challenging than the previous ones, but it is that much more rewarding. This project might seem daunting at first, but I will slowly walk you through it, and together we will create something enlightening!

The design has an Asian aesthetic, with clean, non-fussy lines. The cherry blossom motif further enhances that aesthetic. I have employed the same contrasting elements as seen in the picture frame project, bringing together the curvy flowing lines of the cherry blossom with the rigid straight lines of the shoji-like framework.

The wood I will be using is a nicely figured Western maple. You will need some lighting acrylic, found at any home improvement store, some lamp wiring hardware, including an inline switch; a low watt chandelier light bulb; and some wire strippers. I found my lamp hardware at Wildwood Designs. You will also need a router in a router table with a straight cutting bit to rout the rabbets, or you can chisel it by hand.

CUTTING LIST

Part #	Amount	Part Name	Measurement	Material
1	4	Side Panels	¼" x 5" x 8" (6mm x 127mm x 203mm)	Western maple
2	4	Legs	¾" x ¾" x 12¾" (19mm x 19mm x 324mm)	Western maple
3	4	Rails	¾" x ¾" x 4½" (19mm x 19mm x 114mm)	Western maple
4	8	Retainers	¼" x ⅜" x 4½" (6mm x 10mm x 114mm)	Western maple
5	1	Cross brace	¼" x 1¼" x 4⁹⁄₁₆" (6mm x 32mm x 116mm)	Baltic birch plywood
6	1	Button	¾" x ⁵⁄₁₆" (19mm x 8mm)	Dowel
7	4	Backers	Cut to fit	Acrylic

Cherry Blossom Accent Lamp pattern

Make 2 copies at 110%

Cherry Blossom Accent Lamp Step-by-Step

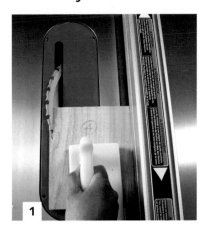

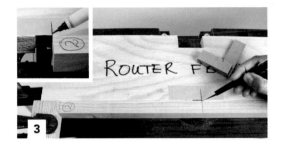

1. Prepare the stock.

Use a table saw with the saw blade tilted at 45° to cut miters onto all edges of parts #1 (sides) and #4 (retainer blanks). Square the blade on the table and proceed to cut the sides to length using the miter gauge equipped with a stop block. Cut the remaining parts, leaving parts #3 (rails), #4 (retainer blank), and #5 (cross brace) to rough length.

2. Number all parts and prepare router.

Number all parts. Leave the lighting acrylic to rough length and width for now. Insert a ¼" (6mm)-diameter straight bit into the router table. Set the router fence flush to the back edge of the router bit. We want a ¼" (6mm)-wide by ¼" (6mm)-deep stopped rabbet in part #2 (the legs)—these rabbets are made to receive parts #1. The rabbet will be 8" (203mm) down from the leg top— the exact length of part #1.

3. Rout the rabbets.

Mark the front edge of the bit on the fence with a steel square (inset). This mark is important; we will not be able to see the bit when we are routing. Make a mark on the leg to indicate the end of the rabbet. Match the end mark on the leg to the mark on the fence. Hold in place and clamp a stop block to the table to ensure the rabbet is the same for all legs.

4. Rout out the stopped rabbets on the legs.

When routing a deep rabbet, make a couple of passes over the router bit until the desired height is met. This will help prevent tear out and will ease strain on the router bit. Carefully but briskly, rout the rabbet until it hits the stop block. Use safety paddles when making each pass.

5. Square the rabbets.

You will notice that the router bit leaves rounded corners on the rabbets. These can easily be squared up by using a very sharp chisel and mallet. Make sure that the piece is clamped to the bench.

Cherry Blossom Accent Lamp Step-by-Step *(continued)*

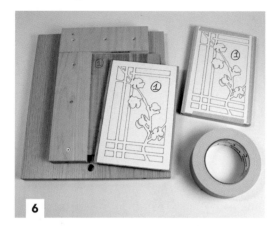

6. Stack the sides.
Use the right-angle alignment jig (see page 192) to stack and properly align each mitered side panel on top of one another. I prefer to stack two side panels at a time—all 4 sides will add up to an uncomfortable 1" (25mm) thickness. You can either use strips of double-sided tape in between the layers or use masking tape on the edges to hold it all in place.

7. Drill blade entry holes.
Equip the drill press with a ⅟₁₆" (2mm)-diameter drill bit and proceed to drill the blade entry holes.

8. Cut out the pattern.
Start by making all interior cuts using a #2 or #5 reverse tooth blade on the scroll saw. Remember to always start in the center with the most delicate cuts and work your way to the perimeter, with the least delicate cuts.

9. Arrange the sides.
Sand the backs of the side panels to get rid of burrs. Arrange the side panels with the miters facing down and tape the edges of the mitered sides together with clear packing tape. Use a straight edge to align the tops of the side panels.

10. Glue the sides.
Flip over the assembly so the miters face up. Brush even layers of wood glue on all miters.

11. Bring sides together.
Fold all sides onto one another and close the assembly with clear packing tape. Before the glue dries, check to see if the assembly is square by measuring the diagonals. If you find that the assembly is not square, place a clamp on the longer diagonal. This will help square up the assembly as the glue dries.

12. Cut the retainers.

I prefer to cut the retainer strips on the scroll saw, as it is the safest method to crosscut such small pieces. Attach a simple pointed guide strip ⅜" (10mm) away from the scroll saw blade (the width of a retainer strip). The guide will help with the blade drift while maintaining an even cut. After one strip is cut, mark for the next strip. You will need eight retainer strips.

13. Cut the notches for the cross brace.

On one set of the retainer strips, position the cross brace in the center and mark the width of the notch for the cross brace. The notch will essentially be 1¼" (32mm) wide by ¼" (6mm) deep. To ensure the notches are properly aligned, stack the two strips with the miters facing toward the inside and attach with double-sided tape. Cut the notches with the scroll saw using a #5 reverse tooth blade.

14. Glue the retainer strips.

Employ the same technique used to glue the sides together. After you are completely satisfied with how the retainer assembly fits into the side assembly, glue the retainer strips using wood glue.

15. Cut the cross brace.

Square one end of the rough-length cross brace. Set the square end flush into one notch of the retainer assembly and place the long end into the other notch. Make a mark on the outside edge where the brace meets the retainer. Finally, cut the brace to length.

16. Glue the dowel piece to the cross brace.

Cut the ¾" (19mm) diameter dowel to ⁵⁄₁₆" (8mm) in length using a manual miter box and back saw. This will become a button to house the ⅜" (10mm) threaded nipple for the lamp wiring. Glue the button in the center of the cross brace with some wood glue. Use a quick clamp to clamp it in place.

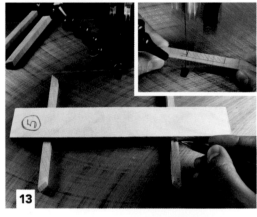

Cherry Blossom Accent Lamp Step-by-Step *(continued)*

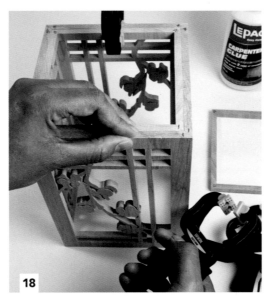

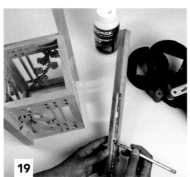

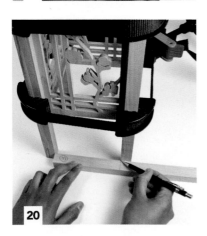

17. Drill rod hole.
After the glue is dry on the cross brace assembly, locate and mark the center of the button. With a 25/64" (10mm) brad point bit, drill a hole through the center of the cross brace assembly.

18. Glue the retainers.
Brush wood glue on the outside edges of the retainer assemblies. Glue the notched retainer on the bottom end of the side panel assembly with the notches facing up. Clamp the retainers in place while the glue sets. After the glue is dry, use a sanding jig (page 189) to flush up the top and bottom.

19. Glue the legs to the side assembly.
Before gluing the legs to the side assembly, pre-sand the inside of each leg. Be sure to maintain square corners and edges. Spread wood glue into the rabbets of the legs and use band clamps to clamp in place.

20. Attach the rails.
Check that the assembly is square. Determine the exact length of the rails. Place a square end of the rail on the inside edge of one leg and make a mark where the other end meets the inside edge of the other leg. Cut the rail to length with a miter saw or table saw. Glue and clamp in place.

21. Apply a finish.
After the glue is dry, sand the entire lamp to a smooth finish using various grits of sandpaper and a sanding block. Soften any sharp corners and edges. Sand the cross brace assembly. Apply three or more coats of a clear protective spray finish. Sand the lamp lightly with 320-grit sandpaper between each coat.

22. Assemble lamp wiring parts.
Assemble all the parts required to wire the lamp hardware: electrical cord with plug and in-line switch, candelabra socket, 1¼" (32mm) threaded nipple, nut and washer, cardboard sleeve (comes with the short hickey), cross brace assembly, wire strippers, screwdriver.

23. Attach the cord to the socket.
Use the wire strippers to strip about ¾" (19mm) off each end of the split cord. Twist the exposed copper wire so it creates a neat bundle. Create an open-ended loop on each bundle. Loop a wire over each screw of the socket. Attach the smooth side of the cord to the gold screw and the textured side of the cord to the silver screw. Tighten the screws.

24. Attach socket assembly to the cross brace assembly.
Insert the socket assembly into the hole of the cross brace. Next, insert the washer and tighten the nut to the underside of the cross brace with a wrench. Finally, slip the protective cardboard sleeve over the socket, covering the screws. Insert and glue the cross brace assembly into the notches of the bottom retainer of the lamp.

25. Glue the acrylic panels.
Cut the acrylic panels to fit by using a very sharp utility knife. Do this by making a few scoring cuts and snapping the panel off along the score line. Spread some silicone glue around the perimeter of each panel. Insert each panel and press into place. Attach nonslip pads under the lamp and insert a chandelier bulb that is no more than 25 watts.

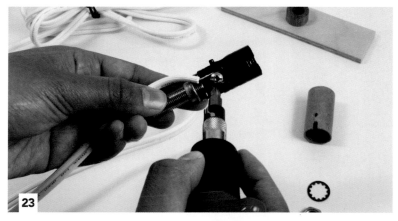

orchid accent lamp

The alternate lamp design is, again, based on my love of orchids. I have employed the same design guidelines as seen in the Cherry Blossom lamp design. The Orchid lamp will also beautifully complement your Orchid picture frame (page 56). The nice thing about my designs is that you can play around with them and make sets that are alike or completely different. Make these collections to add function to your home and office and to illuminate the space. I have chosen to stain this lamp, and there are a couple steps that you should keep in mind if you, too, decide to do the same. Before you glue and assemble the mitered side panels, pre-stain the parts first. Simultaneously, you should also stain the inside edges of the legs and the inside edges of the rails—basically any part that you think will be difficult to stain properly once the lamp is glued and assembled. When you are ready to glue the parts, tape all likely areas with painter's masking tape to prevent excess glue squeeze-out. For example, you might want to tape the inside edges where the legs meet the side panels.

Orchid Accent Lamp pattern
Make 2 copies at 125%

CHAPTER 4
wall accents

The following chapter contains my wall accent series. I have approached each project a little differently, be it in shape or size. The first project is a large square made up of four smaller squares. This is an interesting design to play with—you can incorporate symmetry in a variety of ways. The next projects are based on large circle fretwork designs. We also experiment with Plexiglas acrylic materials in this chapter with some designs that I call tattoo wall art. By using clear acrylic, the design itself can be incorporated with the paint color of the walls in your home. The unique layered wall accent projects use multiple layers of wood to lend a different feel to the pieces. Finally, there are two projects with emphasis on detailed fretwork designs, residing in beautifully simple frames. Whether you are looking for a piece to feature as the center of your décor or a beautiful accessory to brighten up a corner, you'll find a project here.

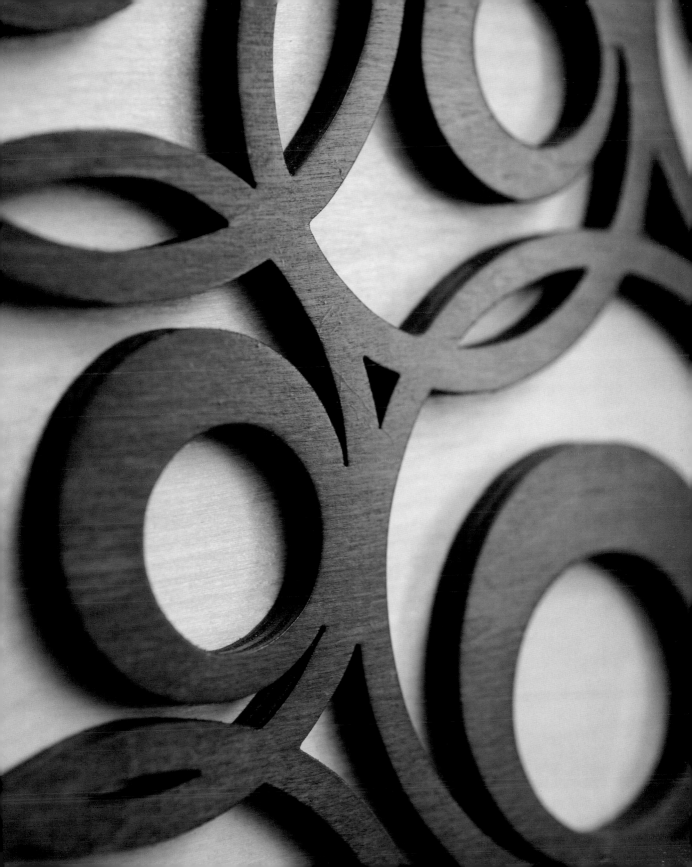

four-piece square

TOOLS & MATERIALS

- Table saw
- Drill press
- Hand drill
- Drill bit, 1/16" (2mm) diameter
- Scroll saw blades, reverse tooth #5
- Clamps
- Spray adhesive
- Wood glue
- Glue roller
- Brad point bit, 3/8" (10mm) diameter
- Spray finish
- Stain
- Veneer tape
- Glue gun
- Glue sticks
- Clear packing tape
- Utility knife
- Hammer
- Sandpaper (150-220 grits)

This project, not unlike the candle holder (page 66), will consist of four individual 8" (203mm) squares brought together to reveal one dynamic art piece. The highly stylized koi fish design resembles the shape of the yin and yang symbol often seen in Chinese culture. The koi fish is a symbol of good fortune, and it is also associated with perseverance and courage. The yin and yang represents contradictions, such as the positive and negative forces found in any single thing.

The key to this project is to have perfectly square cuts, because each square will be laminated from two pieces, which we will accurately align utilizing the right-angle alignment jig. This project is very easy to make, right down to the hanging system that will be used. All you will need is a 3/8" (10mm) brad or Forstner bit. This stunning project will surely leave a lasting impression!

CUTTING LIST

Part #	Amount	Part Name	Measurement	Material
1	4	Tops	1/4" x 8" x 8" (6mm x 203mm x 203mm)	Baltic birch plywood
2	4	Backers	1/2" x 8" x 8" (13mm x 203mm x 203mm)	Baltic birch plywood

Koi Four-piece Square pattern, Head
Make 1 copy at 135%

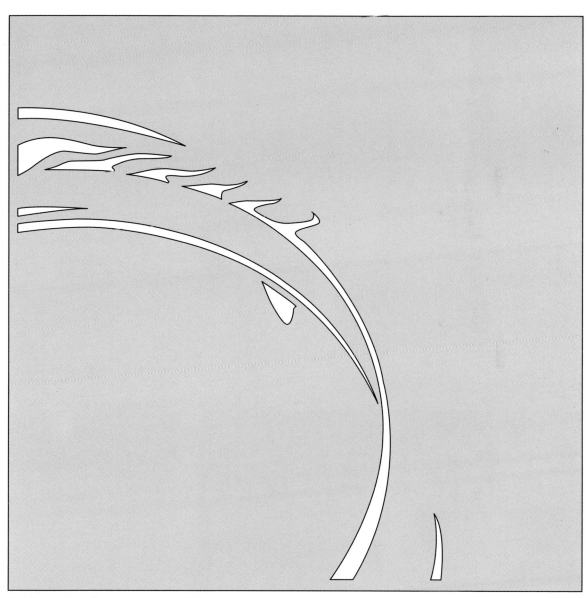

Koi Four-piece Square pattern, Tail
Make 1 copy at 135%

Koi Four-Piece Square Step-by-Step

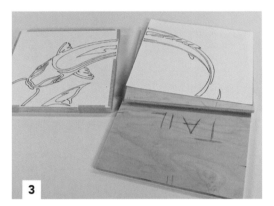

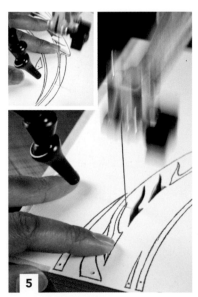

1. Cut all parts on a table saw.
First, cut/rip a fresh edge on the stock using the table saw fence. Rip the stock to the final width, also using the fence, thus creating two parallel edges. It is important to crosscut one end of the board square using the miter gauge. Finally, use the miter gauge with a stop block to crosscut each piece to final length. Each time you will be registering the parallel edge on the miter gauge fence.

2. Lay out parts.
As accuracy is very important, cut the paper pattern (one head and one tail) with a utility knife right on the outline. Lay out the ¼" (6mm)-thick tops so the grain flows correctly, and mark each part. Match up the pattern corners to the square top blanks and attach with spray adhesive.

3. Stack matching parts.
Rotate the two bottom squares (the patternless pieces) 180° to maintain the grain orientation. Stack the matching square parts and use strips of masking tape on the edges. I use the aid of the right-angle alignment jig to carefully align each stack (see picture frame project, page 60) before taping the edges.

4. Drill blade entry holes.
Drill blade entry holes using a 1/16" (2mm) drill bit in a drill press. Be sure to sand the backs of each stack to remove any burrs that may cause difficulty when cutting out the pattern on the scroll saw.

5. Cut out the pattern.
Cut out the pattern using a #5 or bigger reverse tooth blade. Take extra care when cutting the single kerf lines (veining) of the pattern.

6. Stain top of backer parts.
Separate the stacks by removing the tape. Sand all parts with various grits of sandpaper from 150 to 220 grit. Also, remove any burrs or dust from the back and front of the cutout parts. After removing all dust and grit, stain only the tops of the backer parts to desired color. My choice of color is a rich rosewood stain.

7. Prepare the jig.
To aid in perfect alignment of the top and bottom squares, use the invaluable right-angle alignment jig (see page 192). Put the first stained bottom piece in the jig.

8. Glue top cutouts to stained backers.
Carefully roll an even amount of glue on the undersides of the top cutouts. Then, carefully place the top, right side up, onto the backer, which is already situated in the jig.

9. Clamp the parts.
Use scrap wood as a glue block to clamp parts in place. Make sure to elevate the jig, using anything handy so the clamps have enough clearance.

10. Veneer exposed plywood edges.
After the glue is dry, sand all edges of the square assemblies flush. Use an iron set at the cotton setting (no steam!) to apply the veneer tape to all exposed plywood edges. Use a veneer J-roller or scrap wood to apply pressure to fully adhere the tape. Carefully trim the excess veneer using a sharp utility knife. Use a file to flush up the edges of the veneer. Sand lightly.

11. Drill hole for hanging.
On the back of each assembled square, number according to wall orientation. Draw an arrow to indicate which way is up. Mark the location for the hole 1¼" (32mm) down and centered. Set the depth of the drill bit to half the thickness of the piece. Use a ⅜" (10mm) diameter Forstner or brad point bit to drill the hole. Take extra care not to drill through the front of the piece.

12. Finish the squares.
Place each of the squares onto the drying rack (corkboard and toothpicks) and apply several coats of spray finish of choice. Allow drying time between each coat and sand lightly before the next coat is applied.

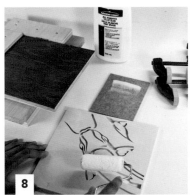

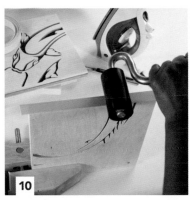

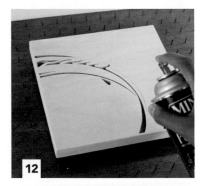

Hanging the Project

A level comes in handy for hanging the four-piece square. Space the pieces so that there is about ¼" between them.

circles four-piece square

The alternate pattern for the four-piece square project is chock-full of circles. It has a vintage appeal with these repeating circle motifs. The pattern for this one is basically the same square rotated four different ways. Look at the layout diagram (below) for the arrangement. Follow the koi four-piece square steps. The only difference is that you will be using the same pattern on both stacks. I used a dark walnut stain on the top pieces and left the backer pieces natural to further enhance the vintage effect.

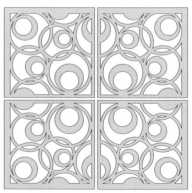

Layout Diagram

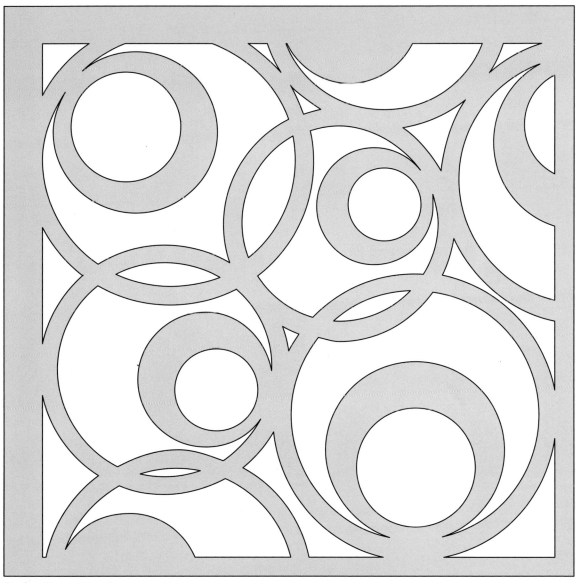

Circles Four-piece Square pattern

Make 2 copies at 135%

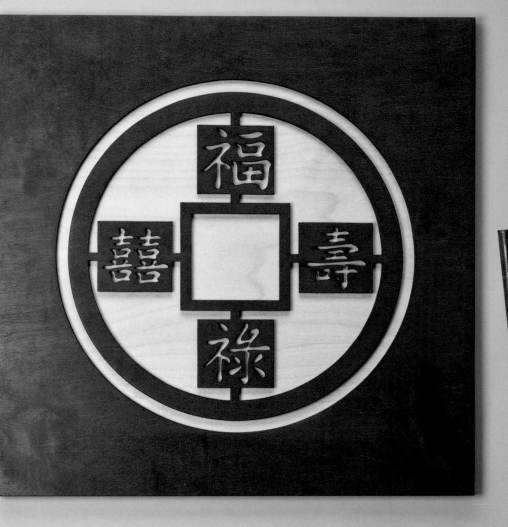

circled wall art

TOOLS & MATERIALS

- Table saw
- Drill press
- Drill bit, ⅟₁₆" (2mm)
- Forstner bits, ⅜" and ⅝" (10mm and 16mm)
- Random orbit sander
- Sanding drum attachment for the drill press, or a disc sander
- Scroll saw blades, reverse tooth #5
- Wood glue
- Sandpaper, various grits
- Glue roller
- Clamps
- Offset wheel/washer, ½" (13mm) radius
- Pencil
- Measuring tape
- Ruler
- Stain/dye of choice
- Finish of choice
- Foam brush
- Iron
- Veneer tape, ¾" (19mm) birch
- Veneer J-roller or scrap block of wood
- Utility knife
- File
- Keyhole hanger
- Chisels, ½" and 1" (13mm and 25mm) width

A circle represents infinity, with no beginning or end. It also gives us a feeling of wholeness and unity. My design is based on an ancient Chinese coin. Its circular shape represents heaven, and the square opening in the center represents earth. It is believed that this unity brings prosperity and an abundance of wealth. I have paired the shape of the coin with four Chinese characters that form an important blessing for any household. The coin is read in the following order: the top character means "good fortune"; the bottom means "prosperity"; the right means "longevity"; and the left means "double happiness." I have also framed the coin with a circular opening, further enhancing the shapes of the piece. This is absolutely a dynamic project that deserves a place of prominence in your home—I hope it brings you good fortune!

CUTTING LIST

Part #	Amount	Part Name	Measurement	Material
1	1	Coin blank	¼" x 14¼" x 14¼" (6mm x 362mm x 362mm)	Baltic birch
2	1	Frame panel	¼" x 19" x 19" (6mm x 483mm x 483mm)	Baltic birch
3	1	Backer panel	½" x 19" x 19" (13mm x 483mm x 483mm)	Baltic birch

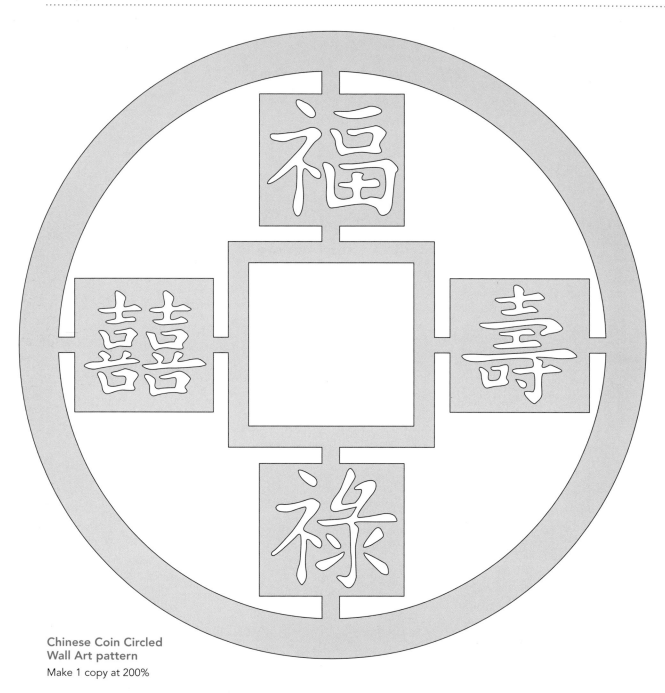

**Chinese Coin Circled
Wall Art pattern**
Make 1 copy at 200%

Chinese Coin Circled Wall Art Step-by-Step

1. Prepare stock.
Cut all parts on the table saw. Number parts accordingly (see cutting list). For this project, I have chosen Baltic birch plywood for stability because the parts are larger.

2. Drill blade entry holes.
After attaching the paper pattern with spray adhesive, drill the blade-entry holes with a ¹⁄₁₆" (2mm) drill bit in the drill press. Be sure to place a scrap backer piece on the drill press table.

3. Cut out the pattern.
Remove all burrs from the back of the coin blank with sandpaper. Begin cutting out the pattern using a #5 reverse tooth blade. Begin with the characters. Proceed to cut out the geometric shapes from the center outward.

4. Cut out the shape.
When all the interior cuts are complete, cut out the circular shape of the coin. Cut as close to the line as possible. If you are not too comfortable with doing that, cut out the rough shape, leaving approximately ¹⁄₃₂" to ¹⁄₁₆" (1mm to 2mm) all around.

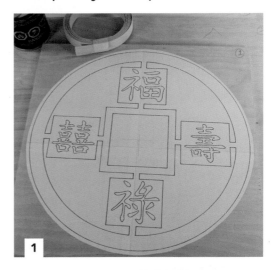

Chinese Coin Circled Wall Art Step-by-Step *(continued)*

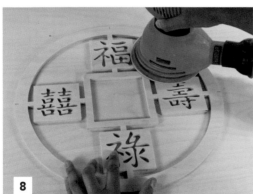

5. Sand the shape.

Sand the coin to its final shape. To clean up any bumps, use either a disc sander or a drum sander attached to the drill press. Adjust the spindle speed of the drill press: 750 rpm for soft wood and 1500 rpm for hard wood. Make an auxiliary table with a hole in the center slightly larger than the sanding drum. Seat the sanding drum in the hole and clamp or bolt the auxiliary table to the drill press table. Be aware of the drum rotation. Feed the piece against the rotation of the drum.

6. Mask the offset.

Determine the placement of the hole in the frame panel (the band of contrasting color that appears around the main piece) by positioning the coin in the center of the frame panel. When you are happy with the placement, draw the ½" (13mm) offset by using a washer or an offset wheel gauge with a ½" (13mm) radius. Mark which way is up on the frame panel.

7. Cut out the hole.

Drill a pilot hole close to the outline. Cut out the hole in the center of the frame panel using a #5 reverse tooth blade. Save the center cutout to use as a gluing aid at a later stage. Unless you have a spindle sander, you will have to smooth out the new cutout in the panel by hand.

8. Sand all parts.

Use a random orbit sander to quickly sand all parts to a smooth finish. Take extra care when sanding the coin cutout. Ease or soften the sharp edges of the coin cutout and the center cutout with 220-grit sandpaper.

9. Stain the coin and frame panel.

Apply a stain of your choice to the coin cutout as well as the frame panel. Do not apply stain to the backer part—this provides contrast.

10. Glue.
Align the frame panel onto the backer. Glue and clamp these two parts in place. Use glue blocks on the corners and all sides to clamp down and obtain even pressure.

11. Veneer exposed plywood edges.
After the edges are given a light sanding to flush up any unevenness, iron veneer on all exposed plywood edges. Start with the top and bottom edges of the frame. Remember to use the J-roller. Trim off the excess veneer on the ends first, then along the edges. Veneer the sides of the frame and trim the excess. Apply stain to the veneered edges.

12. Install keyhole hanger.
Locate and drill appropriate holes with Forstner bits to house the keyhole hanger (see page 126).

13. Glue the coin.
Position and glue the coin in the center of the frame. Use the circle cutoff scrap as a gluing block by placing it over the coin and weighting it with something heavy—a box of cat litter, large telephone directories, a bag of soil, a box of magazines or books, etc. After the glue is dry, apply finish of choice. Allow the finish to dry and sand lightly before the next coat is applied. Repeat process to as many coats of finish as desired.

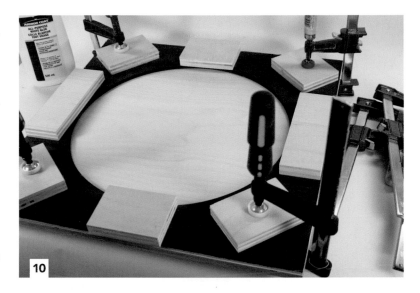

10

11

12

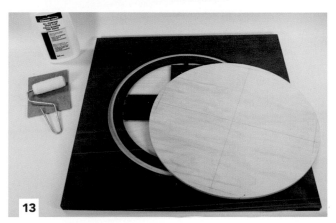

13

tree of life circled wall art

The alternate pattern is a dynamic piece with a true presence. It certainly adds a focal point to any room. The Tree of Life is a symbol of growth and strength, and it connects heaven (with the leaves and branches reaching to the sky) and earth (with deep-reaching roots). This symbol is universally significant in every culture. The only differences between this pattern and the demonstration are the measurements and the use of a deep walnut dye to color the top, which contrasts with the natural backer.

**Tree of Life Circled
Wall Art pattern**
Make 1 copy at 200%

tattooed wall art

TOOLS & MATERIALS

- Drill press
- Drill bit, 1⁄16" (2mm)
- Hand drill
- Scroll saw blades, reverse tooth #5 or choice
- Acrylic sheets
- Utility knife
- Ruler
- Glue stick
- Monofilament fishing line
- Spray adhesive
- Clear packing tape
- Masking tape

Just as the project name suggests, this piece is truly dynamic and unique in many aspects. I wanted to bring a graphic element to a wall in my home while maintaining the wall color for contrast. After contemplating for a while, I came up with the idea of using colorful acrylic sheets—a material that can hold a lot of detail. Acrylic is an unconventional material to cut on the scroll saw, but that is what makes this project so special. So, if you want to try something out of the ordinary with a spectacular result, then this project is for you!

I opted for a nice red opaque color for the leaf motif. The color red means different things to different people; in the Chinese culture, it is a color of good luck and happiness. I soon found out that I needed to strengthen the leaf cutout—it was too fragile to hang on the wall by itself. I then came up with the idea of gluing the piece to a clear acrylic backing using specialty plastic adhesive. This not only provided strength and maintained the contrast of the wall color, but also finished off the piece nicely. I drilled a couple of holes in the acrylic to thread fishing line through for hanging.

CUTTING LIST

Part #	Amount	Part Name	Measurement	Material
1	1	Cutout	Buddha: 1⁄8" x 11" x 15" (3mm x 279mm x 381mm) Leaf: 1⁄8" x 14" x 17" (3mm x 356mm x 432mm)	Colored acrylic
2	1	Backer	Buddha: 1⁄8" x 15⁷⁄8" x 19¾" (3mm x 403mm x 502mm) Leaf: 1⁄8" x 17¾" x 20" (3mm x 451mm x 508mm)	Clear acrylic

Leaf Tattooed Wall Art pattern
Make 1 copy at 200%

Leaf Tattooed Wall Art Step-by-Step

1. Lay out the enlarged pattern.
Enlarge the pattern either professionally or using the poster setting on your printer. If you use your scanner, you will end up with four printer paper-sized sections. Lay out and number each section accordingly.

2. Cut on the dotted lines.
This and the next step assume that your enlargement of the pattern resulted in four pages that need joined. Shade in the edges that will be cut off. Cut off the inside vertical edge of sections 2 and 4 using a utility knife and a straight edge.

3. Paste sections together.
Paste section 2 to 1 with a glue stick. Paste section 4 to 3. Finally, trim the bottom edge of the top assembly (1 and 2) and paste onto the bottom assembly.

4. Assemble materials.
For this project, we will use a ⅛" (3mm)-thick clear acrylic panel for the backing and a ⅛" (3mm)-thick opaque red acrylic panel for the pattern. Keep the protective film on the acrylic until you are required to remove it. You will also need some monofilament fishing line for hanging the piece on the wall.

1

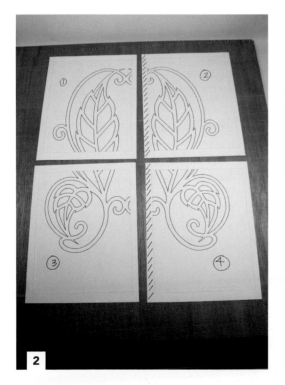

2

3

4

Leaf Tattooed Wall Art Step-by-Step *(continued)*

5. Attach the paper pattern.
Attach the assembled pattern to the acrylic panel using spray adhesive. Remember to leave the protective film in place for now. Attach a couple of strips of clear packing tape on top of the pattern. This will help prevent friction and will produce a smoother cut.

6. Drill the blade entry holes.
Use the drill press, equipped with a 1⁄16" (2mm) or larger drill bit. To get a clean hole without a raised rim around the holes on the back of the acrylic, lower the spindle speed on your drill press and ensure you are using a sharp bit. If you find that the throat depth of your drill press is too shallow (you can't reach the center of the acrylic), switch to a handheld drill to finish drilling the holes.

7. Cut out the pattern.
Use the scroll saw to cut out the pattern with a #5 reverse-tooth blade. Begin in the center and work your way out. Remember to leave the bigger surfaces until the end to cut out.

8. Cut out the final shape.
After all the interior cuts have been made, insert a fresh #5 blade into your scroll saw and proceed to cut out the final shape of the pattern. To achieve a nice, consistent thickness around the perimeter of the pattern, cut either on the inside or the outside of the outline thickness.

> **Scrolling Acrylic**
>
> To prevent the acrylic from melting into itself during scrolling, use a slower speed and steady feed, not too fast or too slow. For safety, use the dust blower of the scroll saw and wear a dust mask!

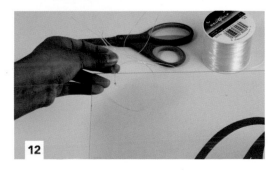

9. Position the cutout on a clear backer.

Remove the protective film from the top of the clear acrylic backer panel. Also, remove the protective film from the back of the leaf cutout. Position the cutout in the center of the clear acrylic backer. Mark the location with masking tape. Ensure both surfaces are free of dust and debris before you glue the pieces together.

10. Glue the cutout to the clear backer panel.

When you are satisfied with the placement of the cutout, spot glue the back of the cutout with glue formulated for acrylic. Use the glue sparingly so that it does not squeeze out. Press the cutout firmly in place. Cover the assembly with a flat piece of wood and something heavy. Allow the assembly to cure for at least 24 hours.

11. Drill hanger holes.

After the glue is set, place masking tape in the top corners of the assembly. Mark out the location for the holes about ¾" (19mm) from the top of the clear panel and about 1" (25mm) from the sides of the panel. Use a ⅟₁₆" (2mm)-diameter drill bit to make the holes. Use a scrap backing piece to prevent chip out on the back of the acrylic.

12. Tie the fishing line.

Remove the protective film from the back of the clear panel. Use a desired length of fishing line and loop the ends of the line through the drilled holes. Use the tails of the loops to tie a secure knot on each end. The piece is now ready to hang in a prominent area on your wall.

buddha tattooed wall art

The alternate pattern is a serene Buddha design. The meaning of the word Buddha is "awakened." It is said that Buddha is the truly enlightened one as to the nature of things. This design differs from the leaf motif in size and color. Please see pattern for measurements. I have chosen to use black opaque acrylic to further enhance the design. With the clear acrylic backing, it appears as if the Buddha is floating. This piece will truly be an inspirational addition to your home.

Buddha Tattooed Wall Art pattern
Make 1 copy at 200%

layered wall art

TOOLS & MATERIALS

- Table saw
- Drill press
- Scroll saw blades, reverse tooth #5
- Drill bit, ⅟₁₆" (2mm)
- Forstner bit, ⅜" and ⅝" (10mm and 16mm)
- Wood screws, #4, ⅜" (10mm)
- Hand drill
- Utility knife
- Spray adhesive
- White glue
- Stain or dye of choice
- Spray finish
- Clamps
- Masking tape
- Ruler
- Foam brush
- Sandpaper (various grits)
- Palm sander
- Keyhole hanger
- Chisels, ½" and 1" (13mm and 25mm) width
- Mallet

The following project is unique among the other projects we have done so far. I was experimenting with depth and how to achieve it in an easy-to-understand and easy-to-execute manner. The final effect I was left with was a stunning visual treat, with all the different layers creating different visual planes. The horse design was simply an enlargement of my Chinese zodiac series, which translated nicely into layered wall art. This project is very simple and the demonstration is straightforward, if you keep all the parts and layers organized. I simply mark or number each part accordingly. For adding contrast to make the cutout pop, I stain or dye the backer pieces. Please note that the middle layer does not have a backer piece, because the bottom cutout layer will serve as its backer.

CUTTING LIST

Part #	Amount	Part Name	Measurement	Material
1	1	Bottom layer	⅛" x 7¼" x 14⅝" (3mm x 184mm x 372mm)	Baltic birch
2	1	Bottom backer layer	½" x 7¼" x 14⅝" (13mm x 184mm x 372mm)	Baltic birch
3	1	Middle layer	⅛" x 3⅝" x 12⅞" (3mm x 92mm x 327mm)	Baltic birch
4	1	Top layer	⅛" x 1 ¹⁵⁄₁₆" x 9¹¹⁄₁₆" (3mm x 49mm x 246mm)	Baltic birch
5	1	Top layer backer	⅛" x 1 ¹⁵⁄₁₆" x 9¹¹⁄₁₆" (3mm x 49mm x 246mm)	Baltic birch
	1	Shims	⅛" (3mm)	

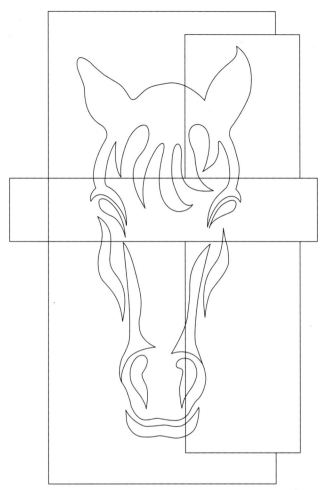

Horse Layered Wall Art, Assembly drawing

Horse Layered Wall Art, Top pattern, Part #4
Make 1 copy at 200%

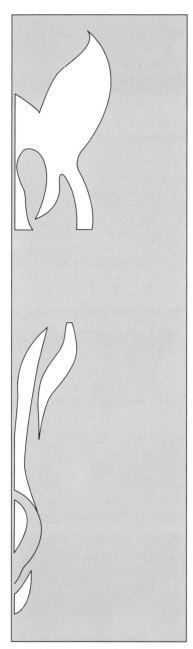

Horse Layered Wall Art,
Middle pattern, Part #3

Make 1 copy at 200%

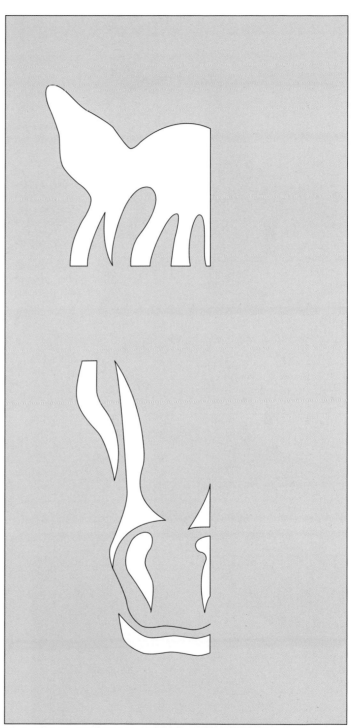

Horse Layered Wall Art, Bottom pattern, Part #1

Make 1 copy at 200%

Horse Layered Wall Art Step-by-Step

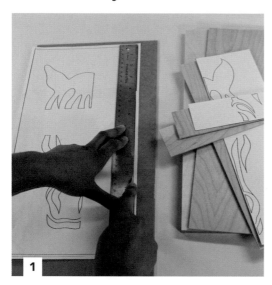

1. Prepare patterns and stock.
Begin by cutting and numbering all the parts—both the wood parts and paper patterns. It is crucial to keep everything organized. Carefully cut out each paper pattern along the perimeter with a sharp utility knife to squarely fit each part.

2. Adhere patterns to appropriate parts.
Attach the paper patterns to matching parts with spray adhesive. Tape the scrap backings to each part with painter's tape. Use a drill press to drill the blade-entry holes for each part.

3. Cut out the bottom layer (Part #1).
Begin scrolling the patterns, starting with the bottom layer. Use a #5 reverse-tooth blade for best results. Start with the curviest line (the horse's mane).

4. Cut out the middle layer (Part #3).
Next, scroll out the middle layer. Pay close attention to the veining around the horse's snout. Take note not to go beyond the edge. Stop approximately ⅛" (3mm) and then reverse the blade carefully to complete the cutout.

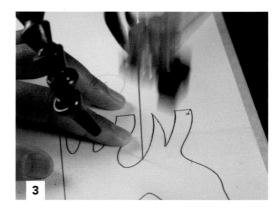

5. Cut out the top layer (Part #4).

Finally, cut out the pattern for the top layer.

6. Mask off bottom layer.

After all parts have been cut out and sanded to a smooth finish, lay out all the layers, including the backers. Mark the area of the bottom layer where the middle layer will overlap. Using painters' tape, mask out the areas outside of this overlap. Burnish the tape to make sure it is adhered fully.

7. Stain the backers.

After masking off the bottom layer, carefully stain the overlap area by brushing the stain/dye toward the center and away from the edges of the tape. This prevents the stain/dye from seeping under the tape. Also stain the bottom layer backer (#2) and the top layer backer (#5).

8. Glue the backers.

After the stain/dye is dry, carefully remove the painter's masking tape from the bottom layer. With the aid of the trusty right-angle jig, roll an even layer of white glue to the underside of the bottom layer and top layer. Align and clamp each part to the matching backer. Do not attach the middle layer just yet.

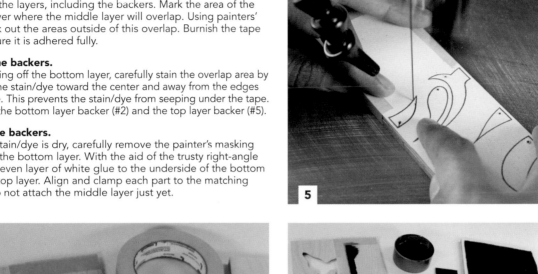

Horse Layered Wall Art Step-by-Step *(continued)*

9. Drill holes for the keyhole hanger.
Locate the hanger approximately 1¼" (32mm) down from the top of the assembly (to the top of the hanger). Position the hanger on the center mark and trace the outline of the hanger. Place a mark ⁵⁄₁₆" (8mm) from the bottom as well as the top edges of the hanger. These marks will be used to drill initial holes for the keyhole hangers. Equip the drill press with a ⅝" (16mm)-diameter Forstner bit and set the depth to approximately ⅛" (3mm) below the surface of the assembly. Make overlapping clearance holes to fit the outline of the hanger, starting with the ⁵⁄₁₆" (8mm) marks made earlier.

10. Square the sides.
Use a 1" (25mm) sharp chisel to square the side of the opening by carefully utilizing a paring motion. Use a mallet for tough woods (a dear friend of mine made the pictured mallet out of recycled wood). Use a smaller chisel to remove wood from within the clearance hole. When the sides have been squared, check the hanger for fit. When you are satisfied, mark the center opening of the hanger onto the clearance opening.

11. Drill holes for hanger.
A few ⅜" (10mm) clearance holes are required in the center of the opening in order to accommodate the screw head for hanging. Equip the drill press with a ⅜" (10mm) Forstner bit and carefully drill overlapping holes approximately ⅛" (3mm) deep just beyond the pencil mark. Square up the edges. When you are completely satisfied with the fit of the hanger, drill screw holes and use #4, ⅜" (10mm)-long screws to affix the hanger.

12. Assemble the layers.
A few ⅛" (3mm)-thick shims are required under the top layer. This prevents the top layer from racking or breaking off. Begin by locating and gluing the middle layer to the bottom layer. Glue a couple of shims to the bottom layer before the final gluing of the top layer. Apply finish of choice when the glue is dry.

butterfly layered wall art

The alternate pattern is a beautiful butterfly design. Butterflies are a favorite subject of mine. They are gracefully fragile, yet heartily strong. The difference with this pattern is again the color I chose, which is a rich red mahogany stain for the backer pieces. The other difference is the dimensions. Please see the pattern for measurements. Of course you could also scale this pattern to your liking. Remember to use shims to level and strengthen the top layer.

Butterfly Layered Wall Art, Assembly drawing

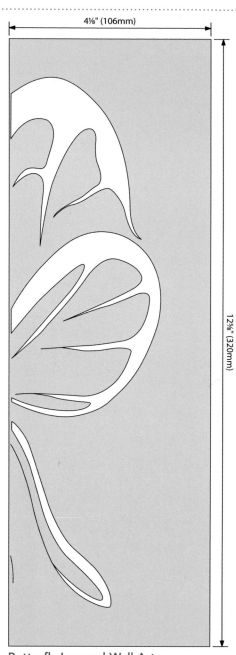

4⅛" (106mm)

12⅝" (320mm)

**Butterfly Layered Wall Art,
Top pattern, Part #4**

Make 1 copy at 200%

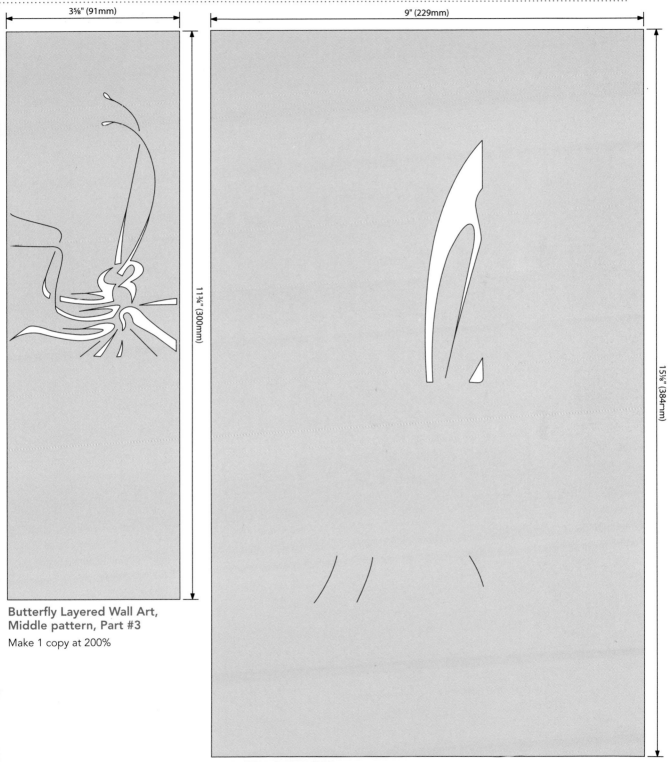

3⅝" (91mm)

11¾" (300mm)

Butterfly Layered Wall Art, Middle pattern, Part #3

Make 1 copy at 200%

9" (229mm)

15⅞" (384mm)

Butterfly Layered Wall Art, Bottom pattern, Part #1

Make 1 copy at 200%

framed wall art

TOOLS & MATERIALS

- Table saw
- Miter saw
- Dado blade (optional)
- Drill press
- Spline slot jig
- Drill bits, ¹⁄₁₆"–⅛" (2mm–3mm) diameter
- Scroll saw blades, reverse tooth #2 and #5
- Wood glue
- Spray adhesive
- Glue gun
- Glue sticks
- Picture hanger wire
- 2 eye hooks
- Stain of choice (optional)
- Clear packing tape
- Band clamps
- Dovetail/utility saw
- Palm sander
- Painter's tape
- Hand drill
- Spray finish
- Sandpaper, 150-320 grits
- Wood screws, #6, ½" (13mm)

This design is based on the mythology of the Green Man. The Green Man represents rebirth and re-growth in the spring and is also the guardian of the forests. The image of this deity is often found in churches, carved in either stone or wood.

My design is highly intricate with lots of twists and turns. After burning through about a half a dozen blades, you will be left with a piece that is delicate in appearance, yet incredibly robust because all the cutouts will cause a web-like effect. The simple gallery-style frame will have mitered corners reinforced with splines. I will discuss how to use a simple shop-made table saw jig to achieve the slots for the splines. The frame members will be made out of Eastern maple. The frame panel, which will sit in a rabbet, will be made out of Baltic birch plywood. You will also need ⅛" (3mm)-thick hardwood for the splines. The frame will hang on picture wire, which will be threaded through some screw eye hooks, purchased at any hardware or framing store. This project is sure to leave you with growing experience!

CUTTING LIST

Part #	Amount	Part Name	Measurement	Material
1	1	Pattern panel	⅛" x 10⅞" x 17" (3mm x 276mm x 432mm)	Baltic birch
2	1	Frame panel	⅜" x 21½" x 28½" (10mm x 546mm x 724mm)	Baltic birch
3	2	Frame sides	¾" x 1¼" x 23" or 20"* (19mm x 32mm x 584mm or 508mm)	Eastern maple
4	2	Frame top/bottom	¾" x 1¼" x 16" or 20"* (19mm x 32mm x 406mm or 508mm)	Eastern maple
	8	Splines for miters	⅛" x 1" x 1½" (3mm x 25mm x 38mm)	Hardwood

* 20" measurements are for the Green Man; alternate measurement is for Quan Yin.

**Green Man Framed
Wall Art pattern**
Make 1 copy at 220%

Green Man Framed Wall Art Step-by-Step

1. Prepare the stock.
Cut out all parts of the frame and pattern panel. Make sure to leave the frame members extra long to receive the miters at a later stage. Also number all parts according to the cutting list.

2. Attach scrap backer.
Attach a scrap backer panel to the pattern panel with some hot glue. Use clamps to keep the assembly in place while tacking each edge.

3. Drill blade-entry holes.
Drill the blade-entry holes by hand using a hand drill because the panel is larger than what most drill presses can accommodate. Try to keep the drill square to the stock to ensure a perpendicular hole. Use a scrap backer.

4. Cut out the pattern.
Carefully cut out the delicate parts of the pattern. Start in the center and work your way to the outside of the piece. When all the interior cuts are complete, cut out the final shape of the piece. It is amazing how strong the web-like delicate parts are within the design.

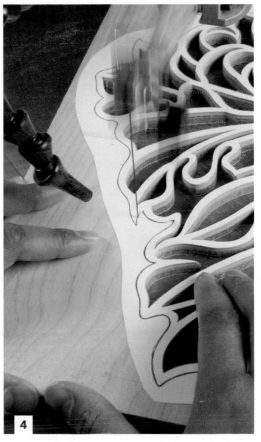

Green Man Framed Wall Art Step-by-Step *(continued)*

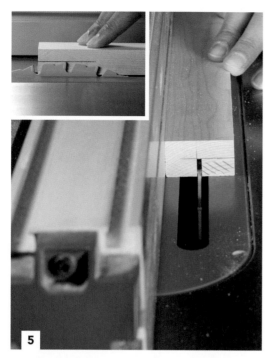

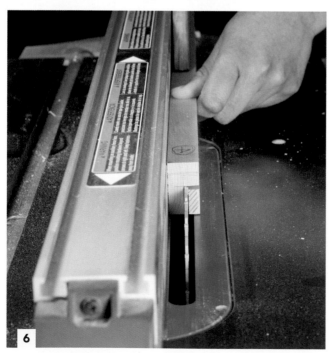

5.

5. Cut the rabbets in the frame members.
Equip the table saw with a rip or combination blade. Cut the rabbets in the frame members/sides. We will be using a single blade, instead of a dado blade, in a two-step process. The rabbet will be ¾" (19mm) deep by ⅜" (10mm) wide. Set the height of the blade. Then, set the distance between the fence and the blade by lining up the layout line with the inside of the blade. Make the cut using a push stick.

6. Final cut for rabbet.
Complete the rabbet by cutting the other side. Readjust the blade height and fence distance. Again, use your layout lines to set adjustments. Remember to use your push stick for safety. Also, set up your cut so that the cutoff falls away from the blade and does not get trapped between the blade and the fence.

7. Cut the miters.
You can cut the miters onto the frame sides, either on the table saw with a miter gauge set to 45° or with a miter saw set at 45°. Cut a miter on one end of each side, top, and bottom first; then, set up a stop block to get the exact same length for each corresponding piece.

8. Assemble the frame.
Before gluing the frame parts, dry fit the pieces and number all corresponding miters. This will ensure a smooth glue up. Spread an even layer of glue on all miters. Bring the pieces together and use a band clamp to easily clamp the frame. Remember to always check for square by measuring diagonally from corner to corner.

7.

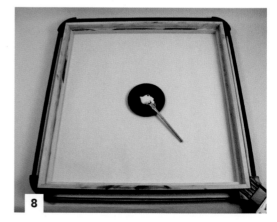

6.

8.

9. Lay out miter splines.

Add splines to strengthen the mitered corners of the frame. First, begin by marking layout lines on one corner of the frame. On the top of the corner of the frame, mark ¾" (19mm) in from each corner, then join the marks with a straight line. This will give you a layout line to set the height of the saw blade.

10. Complete layout of splines.

Mark the thickness of your spline (usually the thickness of your saw blade) on the edge of the frame. I have measured ⁵⁄₁₆" (8mm) from front and back edges of the frame. This will give you layout lines to set the distance between the table saw fence and blade.

11. Cut the spline slots.

To cut the miter spline slots, a simple table saw jig made out of shop scraps is required (page 194). Before cutting the slots, set the height of the blade by using your earlier layout line made on the front of the frame. Set the distance by using the layout lines made on the edge of the frame. Place a corner of the frame in the cradle, hold the frame firmly in place and slide the whole assembly along the fence and over the blade. You will need two slots per corner. Simply flip the frame from front to back to complete the slots (no need to readjust the table saw fence).

12. Glue the splines.

Before gluing the splines into the slots, make sure to test fit each spline first! You may need to adjust the fit of the spline by sanding it down to thickness. After you are satisfied with the fit, glue each spline in place, making sure that the spline is completely bottomed out by pushing it firmly into place. No clamps needed here! Please note that the arrow indicates grain direction of the spline.

13. Trim and flush up the splines.

Use a dovetail or utility hand saw to carefully trim each spline to about ¹⁄₁₆" to ⅛" (2mm to 3mm) away from the edge of the frame. Use a sharp chisel, random orbit sander, or sanding block to flush the splines to the frame.

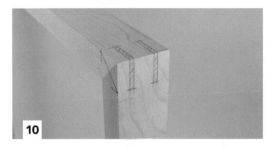

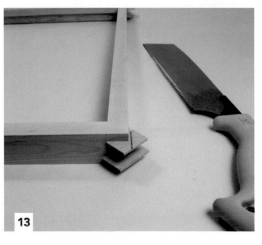

Green Man Framed Wall Art Step-by-Step (continued)

14. Stain the frame and cutout.
Carefully sand the cutout with a sanding block and remove any burrs and fuzz. I opted for a dark walnut stain to finish the piece. Use a large, shallow container filled with stain to dip the cutout piece. Soak up the excess stain by placing the cutout face up onto a couple layers of paper towel. Brush the stain onto the frame.

15. Attach the frame panel.
After you are satisfied with the fit of the frame panel into the frame, sand the panel to a smooth finish with a random orbit sander. Attach the panel to the frame with #6, ½" (13mm) screws. Transfer the width of the rabbet the panel sits on with a pencil. Evenly space the screw holes around the perimeter. Drill countersink holes and screw the panel in place. No glue needed here!

16. Attach the cutout.
Center the cutout in the frame. Once satisfied with the placement, carefully place painter's masking tape along the widest points of the cutout. Roll an even layer of glue onto the back of the cutout and reposition along the tape strips. Use a box filled with heavy items, such as books, to weigh down the cutout as the glue dries.

17. Attach the picture wire.

Spray the entire frame with three or more coats of a clear protective finish. On the back of the frame, mark and drill angled holes approximately a third of the way down from the top of the frame, where the rabbet meets the edge of the frame panel. These holes will receive the eye hooks. I prefer to angle my eye hooks into the rabbet so that the frame will hang more flush against the wall. With the two hooks positioned on either side of the frame, loop one end of the picture wire through the first hook and twist the tail of the wire in place.

18. Finish.

Determine the length of the wire by finding the center of the frame and measuring approximately 1" (25mm) from the top. Use the wire to join the dots and add some extra length to the wire. Snip the wire and loop it through the second eye hook. Twist the wire to finish.

17

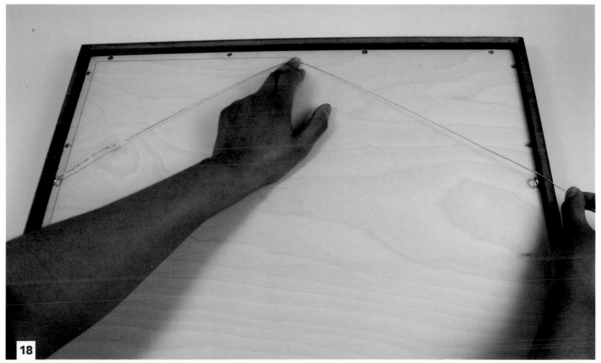

18

goddess of compassion (quan yin) framed wall art

The alternate pattern is a stunning Goddess of Compassion, known as Quan Yin in Chinese culture. Quan Yin is an ancient deity who is the protector of women and has a great love for humankind. She also takes the burdens of the world and makes them her own. The difference with this pattern is the dimensions of all the parts. Please see the pattern for measurements. I also used an ebony dye for the cutout. To further emphasize the design, I dyed the frame members the same color.

Goddess Framed Wall Art pattern
Make 1 copy at 200%

8¾" (222mm)

16½" (419mm)

office accessories

Everyone needs a little organization in his or her life, especially when it comes to the home office. The upcoming few projects will demonstrate how you, too, can achieve a well-organized and exceptionally good-looking workspace. These projects include a simple yet elegant pen holder, a desktop business card holder with surprising utility, a highly functional and striking desktop file holder, a tissue box cover made to add a custom look to your office, and last but not least, a stylish and useful magnet board for everyday reminder notes. You will find all design themes previously explored here in this chapter. By simply adjusting the patterns and scaling as desired, you can have a great custom-designed office collection.

pen holder

TOOLS & MATERIALS

- Table saw
- Drill press
- Drill bits, 1/16" (2mm)
- Wood glue
- White glue
- Glue brush
- Spray adhesive
- Double-sided tape
- Clear packing tape
- Painter's masking tape
- Scroll saw blades, reverse tooth #2/0, #2, and #5
- Finish of choice
- Stain/dye of choice
- Foam brush
- Blue paper towels or cotton rags
- Drying rack
- Measuring tape
- Ruler
- Putty knife
- Felt pads/non-slip bumper pads
- Sandpaper (various grits)
- Clamps
- Iron
- Veneer tape (birch)
- Veneer J-roller
- Utility knife

The first project in the office series is a pen holder, so that you can actually find a pen right at your fingertips when you need it. My design for the pen holder is a continuation of my Organic series—the flowing curvy lines of a flower, contrasted against the rigid straight lines of a framework aesthetic. The calla lily represents magnificence and beauty, which are some of the right attributes for your office. The pen holder is constructed with simple miters cut on the table saw. Your pens will never be without a home again!

I have two alternate designs for you to choose from. The first alternate design is a silhouette of a swallow. Swallows are said to be symbols of health, wealth, loyalty, and the long and hard journey home.

If you are looking to add circles to your office collection, the circles pen holder is for you. To achieve the reflection as seen in the finished piece, simply stack the outer wrap two pieces high so you end up with two stacks. Then attach each opposing pattern to each stack. If you stack all four pieces of the outer wrap and only use one half of the pattern you will not end up with the reflection. That is also perfectly acceptable.

CUTTING LIST

	Part #	Amount	Part Name	Measurement	Material
Outer Wrap:	1	4	Sides	1/8" x 3¼" x 4⅝" (3mm x 83mm x 117mm)	Plywood
Sub-Assembly:	2	4	Sides	¼" x 3" x 4¼" (6mm x 76mm x 108mm)	Plywood
	3	1	Bottom	⅜" x 3" x 3" (10mm x 76mm x 76mm)	Plywood

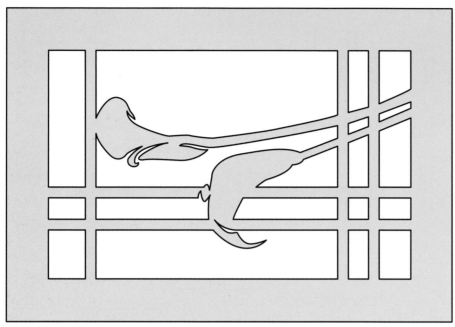

Calla Lily Pen Holder pattern
Make 1 copy at 100%

Bird Pen Holder pattern
Make 1 copy at 100%

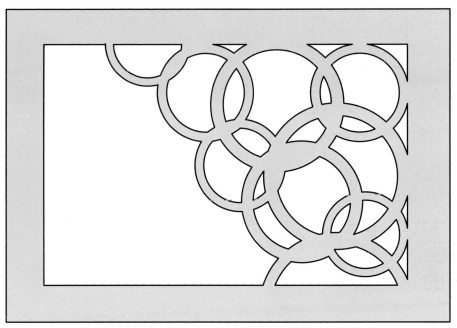

Circles Pen Holder pattern

Make 1 copy at 100%

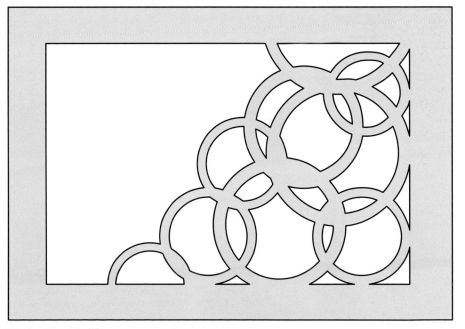

Circles Pen Holder pattern

Make 1 copy at 100%

Calla Lily Pen Holder Step-by-Step

1. Prepare the stock.

Tilt your table saw blade to a 45° angle and cut a miter on one edge of the sub-assembly sides. Adjust the table saw fence to the final width and complete the other edge. Use the miter saw equipped with a stop block to cut the box sides to length.

Attach the sub-assembly sides with clear packing tape. Measure the exact width that the outer wrap sides need to be. Cut the outer wrap sides on the table saw with the tilted saw blade. Finally, tilt the table saw blade back to 90° to cut the outer wrap sides to length and the bottom part to size.

2. Number all parts.

Number each part according to the cutting list as they are cut.

3. Assemble the sides of the sub-assembly.

An easy way to assemble the 4 sides of a mitered box is to use strips of clear packing tape as clamps. Align all the sides miter-to-miter along a straight edge and place strips of tape along each seam (as seen in the Accent Lamp project). Before you glue the sides together, sand the interior to a smooth finish.

4. Apply glue to miters.

Flip the assembly so that the miters are facing up. With a glue brush, apply glue to each miter. Do not forget the outer miters. Wrap each miter onto the next, bringing the last 2 miters together to complete the assembly. Check the assembly for square (see inset).

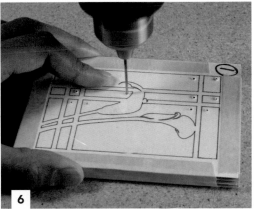

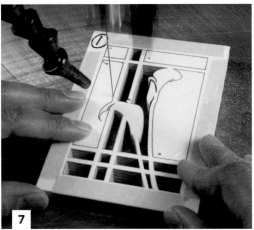

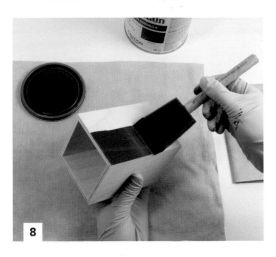

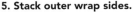

5. Stack outer wrap sides.

While the sub-assembly is curing, start to tackle the outer wrap. Use the indispensible right-angle alignment jig (page 192) to stack the 4 sides of the outer wrap. Use painter's masking tape to attach all pieces of the stack. You can also use strips of double-sided tape in-between the layers of the stack.

6. Drill blade entry holes.

For a smoother cut on the scroll saw, place a few strips of clear packing tape to the top of the stack. Drill blade-entry holes with a ¹⁄₁₆" (2mm) drill bit in your drill press.

7. Cut out the pattern.

Use the scroll saw to cut out the pattern using a #5 reverse tooth blade. Remember to start in the center of the piece and work your way out.

8. Stain the sides of the sub-assembly.

After the glue is dry on the sub-assembly, sand it to a smooth finish while maintaining its squareness. Apply a stain or dye of choice to add contrast to the project. As an alternative, you may choose to stain the outer wrap and maintain the natural color of the sub-assembly to reverse the contrast.

Calla Lily Pen Holder Step-by-Step *(continued)*

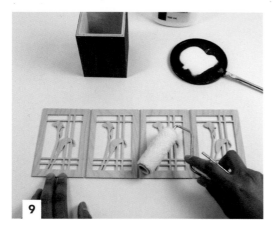

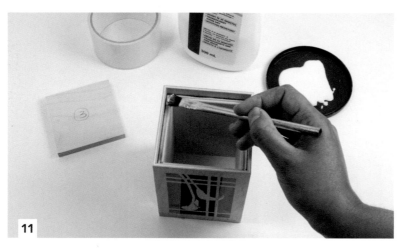

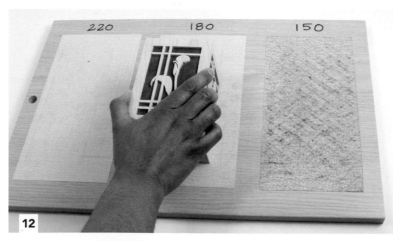

9. Glue outer wrap.
While waiting for the stain on the sub-assembly to dry, carry on with the outer wrap pieces. Clean up the inside of the cutouts by sanding lightly to remove any burrs. Then, as done with the sub-assembly, attach each miter of the outer wrap with clear packing tape. After the stain on the sub-assembly has dried, roll an even layer of white glue to the inside of the outer wrap. Do not forget to apply glue to each of the miters.

10. Attach the outer wrap.
With the outer wrap upside down, wrap the sides around the sub-assembly. Putting the wrap on upside down means that the top of the pen holder will automatically be flush. You will also create a rabbet for the bottom to sit in. Use glue blocks to clamp the sides to the sub-assembly, making sure the two assemblies are well-adhered to one another.

11. Attach the bottom.
Verify that the bottom piece fits squarely into the rabbet before you glue it in place. Brush some wood glue into the rabbet and insert the bottom. Clamp in place.

12. Sand the sides.
After the glue is dry on the final assembly, use the sanding base jig (page 23) with various grits to sand the sides of the assembly to a smooth finish.

13. Flush up the top and bottom.

Use the sanding base to sand the top and bottom of the pen holder flush. This will ready the top edges of the pen holder to receive the veneer tape.

14. Veneer the top edge.

Use the same steps we used to veneer the edges of the key cabinet (page 74)—apply strips, iron them on, then use the J-roller to burnish them. The difference is that we are making a miter joint instead of a butt joint with the veneer. Make sure to line up the miters exactly with the corners of the pen holder.

15. Flush up the edges of the veneer.

Cut the excess veneer with a utility knife. Then, carefully use a file to clean up all the edges of the veneer. Sand the top of the veneer lightly. Apply a clear protective spray finish. Finally, apply some nonslip bumper pads to the bottom of the pen holder.

13

14

15

mokajade designs

"embellishments for your home and person"

www.mokajadedesigns.etsy.com
www.flickr.com/photos/mokajade

roshaan ganief
roshie@shaw.ca
604.805.9241

business card holder

TOOLS & MATERIALS

- Drill press
- Drill bit, 1⁄16" (2mm) diameter
- Scroll saw blades, reverse tooth #2/0, #1, #2, and #5
- Wood glue
- White glue
- Glue sticks
- Glue gun
- Spray adhesive
- Mini quick clamps
- Clear packing tape
- Double-sided tape
- Painter's masking tape
- Veneer tape, birch (optional)
- Veneer J- roller
- Iron
- Sandpaper (various grits)
- Stain/dye of choice
- Shallow container
- Finish of choice
- Utility knife
- Ruler
- Putty knife
- Scrap backer material

Do you need a way to display your business cards in the office or on a display table at a conference or craft show? I have a great solution that is both stunning and travel-friendly: an eye-catching collapsible business card holder. The holder will easily accommodate 70 2"x 3" (51mm x 76mm) business cards. To make the holder collapsible, I had to use a half-lap joint. This joint is simply a deep notch that stops halfway in each mating piece. I will discuss the process of achieving a great-fitting half-lap joint using only your scroll saw. A business card is a great promotional tool, which is a reflection of you as soon as you hand it out to potential customers or clients. Therefore, it needs to be both attractive and professional. A well-crafted and attention-grabbing business card holder that displays these cards will further enhance your credibility as a business professional.

The pattern I will be demonstrating is a striking rose design. The rose represents love in its various forms. The alternate pattern is a variation of the dragonfly design as seen in the belt buckle project.

CUTTING LIST

Part #	Amount	Part Name	Measurement	Material
1	1	Top	1⁄8" x 3¾"x 6⅝" (3mm x 95mm x 168mm)	Baltic birch plywood
2	1	Long backer	¼" x 3¾" x 6⅝" (6mm x 95mm x 168mm)	Baltic birch plywood
3	1	Short cross piece	⅜" x 3¾" x 3½" (10mm x 95mm x 89mm)	Baltic birch plywood

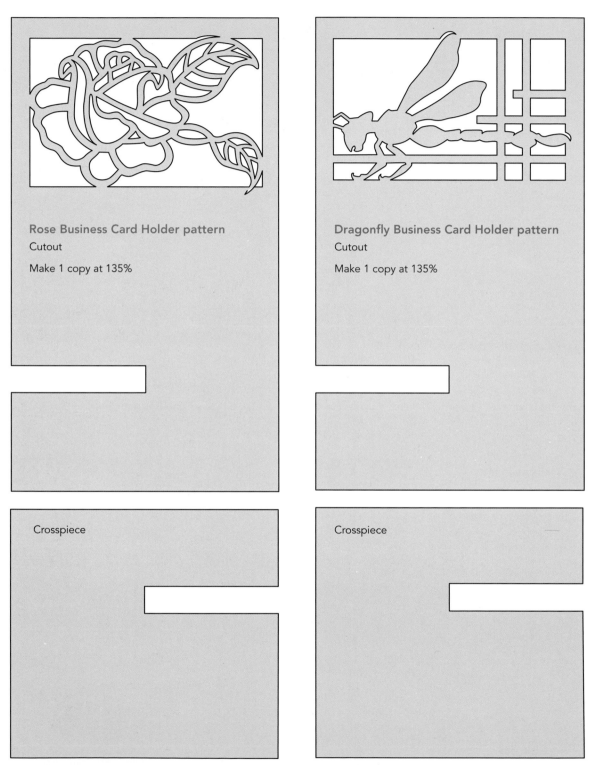

Rose Business Card Holder pattern
Cutout

Make 1 copy at 135%

Dragonfly Business Card Holder pattern
Cutout

Make 1 copy at 135%

Crosspiece

Crosspiece

Rose Business Card Holder Step-by-Step

1. Prepare stock.
Cut out the pieces according to the cutting list—this will make the pieces final size. There are only a few pieces to this project, but it is always good practice to number each individual part. As all parts are cut to final size, it is best to cut out the paper pattern on the outline with a utility knife and ruler. Attach the paper patterns to the appropriate wood parts with temporary spray adhesive. For a smoother cut, apply a few strips of clear packing tape over the paper patterns. Attach scrap backer to top.

2. Attach scrap backer to top.
Using painter's masking tape, attach a piece of scrap backer to the top (Part #1). I am using ¼" (6mm) mahogany plywood as a scrap backer.

3. Cut out the pattern.
After drilling the blade entry holes, use a #2/0 or #1 reverse tooth blade in the scroll saw to cut all interior parts. Remember to always map out your cuts before you make them. Do not get boxed in! Leave the half-lap lines for a later stage.

4. Attach cutout on backer.
After all the interior cuts are made, stack the cutout on the long backer piece. Use a few strips of double-sided tape to temporarily attach the two pieces. Always use the tape sparingly to make separation easier.

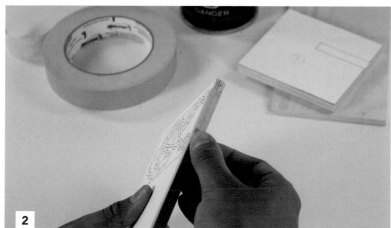

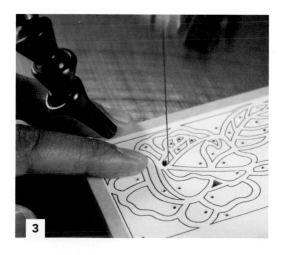

Rose Business Card Holder Step-by-Step *(continued)*

5. Mark the exact thickness of half-laps.
Before cutting the half-laps, sand the pieces smooth, then use a red felt-tip pen to mark out the exact thickness on each mating piece. The lines on the pattern are meant as guidelines, because cutting and sanding may alter the actual measurements. Verify measurements to increase accuracy.

6. Cut the backer piece half-lap.
Use a #5 reverse tooth blade to cut out the half-lap on the top assembly. Try to stay on the inside of the line, as the goal is to leave the entire thickness of the line visible. You can always take more material away, but you can never get the material back! Be sure to test fit the two parts as you go, making minor adjustments as necessary.

7. Cut the short piece half-lap.
After the top assembly has been sanded to a smooth finish, mark the half-lap thickness on the short crosspiece. Use a #5 reverse tooth blade to cut out the half-lap. Test fit the parts, and make necessary adjustments.

8. Separate the stack.
After you are satisfied with the fit, promptly separate the stack. It is important to mark each mating piece, especially when making several business card holders at a time. Use a wide putty knife to carefully separate the top from the backer. If desired, apply veneer to the exposed edges of the crosspiece.

9

10

11

12

9. Stain the parts before gluing.
Sand all parts to a smooth finish and focus on removing any burrs. Apply a stain to the cutout and short crosspiece by dipping them in a tray filled with the desired stain. Only apply the stain on the back side of the backer piece in order to create contrast on the front.

10. Attach the cutout and backer piece.
After the stain is dry, use a glue roller to roll an even layer of white glue on the back of the cutout only. Position and clamp the cutout to the backer piece, making sure to align the slots properly. Use the right-angle alignment jig for perfect alignment.

11. Apply veneer tape to exposed plywood edges.
After all edges have been sanded square, apply veneer tape to any exposed plywood edges. Of course, this step is not necessary, but it certainly finishes everything off nicely. Trim the excess veneer flush with a utility knife.

12. Finish.
Carefully stain any unfinished edges. Apply a protective finish of choice. The great thing about this business card holder is that it is meant to be collapsible, so there's no need to glue the pieces together.

file organizer

TOOLS & MATERIALS

- Table saw
- Dado blade
- Drill press
- Drill bits, 1/16" (2mm) diameter
- Scroll saw blades, reverse tooth #5
- Glue sticks
- Glue gun
- Wood glue
- White glue
- Glue roller
- Spray adhesive
- Utility knife
- Clamps
- Mini quick clamps
- Clear packing tape
- Masking tape
- Sandpaper (various grits)
- Random orbit sander (or sanding block)
- Stain/dye (of choice)
- Finish (of choice)
- Veneer tape (birch)
- Veneer J-roller
- Iron
- Putty knife
- File
- Nonslip bumper pads/felt pads

If you are like most people, chances are you have a stack of unsightly files on your desk. To help curb this habit, I have come up with a simple, yet striking, desktop file holder solution. The file organizer will hold files vertically with dividers to organize it more efficiently.

The pattern I will demonstrate is a floating circles design. The circles are unwillingly contained with straight lines to add visual contrast. Like the business card holder, the file holder can also be taken apart when not in use. This is achieved by cutting notches or dadoes into the rails and corresponding shallow notches into the dividers. The materials I will be using are Baltic birch plywood with veneered edges for the dividers, and solid maple for the rails. The simple yet elegant profile cut into the rails adds an Asian aesthetic to the overall look of the file holder. Stacked files will soon be a thing of the past with this attractive and functional file holder.

CUTTING LIST

Part #	Amount	Part Name	Measurement	Material
1	2	Pattern panels	1/8" x 6" x 9" (3mm x 152mm x 229mm)	Baltic birch
2	2	Backer panels	1/8" x 6" x 9" (3mm x 152mm x 229mm)	Baltic birch
3	3	Divider panels	1/8" x 6" x 9" (3mm x 152mm x 229mm)	Baltic birch
4	2	Runners	3/4" x 3/4" x 10 1/4" (19mm x 19mm x 260mm)	Solid maple

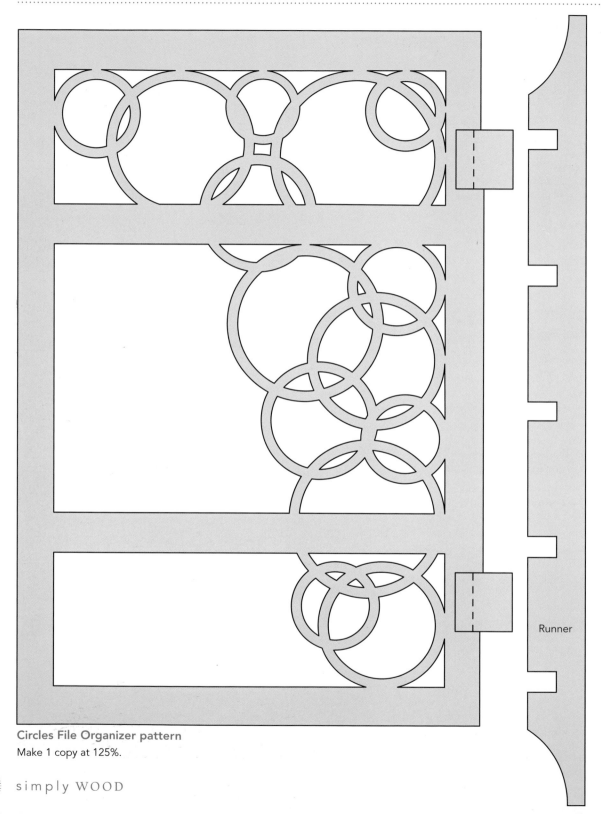

Runner

Circles File Organizer pattern
Make 1 copy at 125%.

Circles File Organizer Step-by-Step

1. Prepare the stock.
Use a table saw to cut all parts to final length and width with a combination blade. A combination blade is a great choice since we are both ripping and crosscutting at the same time. Number each part accordingly as it is cut.

2. Stack the parts.
Use a ruler and utility knife to cut the paper pattern to exact size. Use a spray adhesive to adhere the paper pattern to the parts. With the aid of our trusty right-angle alignment jig (page 192), stack the two pattern panels and align. Attach the stack with masking tape or a few strips of double-sided tape.

3. Drill the blade entry holes.
Use a 1/16" (2mm)-diameter drill bit in the drill press to drill appropriate blade entry holes. Always use a fresh scrap backer to drill into. Sand away any burrs left behind on the back of the stack.

1

2

3

Circles File Organizer Step-by-Step (continued)

4. Cut out the pattern.
Use your blade of choice to cut out the pattern on the scroll saw. This pattern, like some previous ones, has many sharp inside corners. Round the corners a bit and then go back and square the corners. With cutting circles, the one thing to remember is to keep turning your workpiece in a smooth motion to avoid lumps or bumps.

5. Sand the parts.
With all the interior cuts complete, separate the stack by removing the masking tape. Sand all the divider panels, including the cutout panels and backer panels. You can use either a random orbit sander or sanding block with various grits of sandpaper to sand to a smooth finish.

6. Attach cutout panels to backer panels.
Use your stain or dye of choice to color the top of the backer panels. This will add contrast. Use the right-angle alignment jig to precisely align and glue the cutout to the backer panel. Use a glue roller to roll an even layer of white glue on the back of the cutout part only, then clamp to the backer. Repeat for the second cutout and backer.

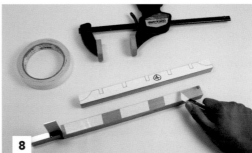

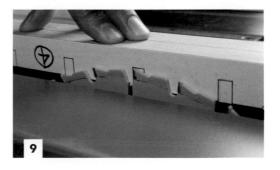

7. Veneer exposed edges.

Remove any glue squeeze-out on edges of panel assemblies. Use an iron to glue the top and side edges of all panels (no need to veneer the bottom edge). Since the veneer tape is ¾" (19mm) wide and the panels are only ¼" (6mm) wide, cut the veneer strips in half down their length.

8. Prepare the runners.

With the runners cut to exact length, attach the runner paper pattern to one runner. Join the 2 runners with strips of double-sided tape. Make sure to align their edges as well as their ends. Use some clamp pressure to fully adhere the runners.

9. Prepare for notches in the runners.

Since the lines on the runner paper pattern are only guides, it is best to use these guides to mark the exact thickness of the panels. Hold the panel against the guidelines and mark the exact width. Next, use the runners to set the height of the blade. Then, set the distance between the blade and the stop block.

Circles File Organizer Step-by-Step *(continued)*

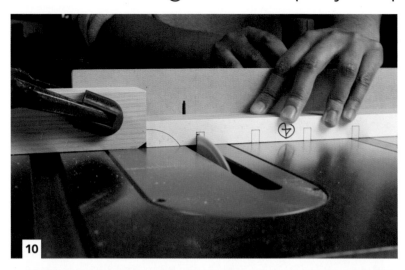

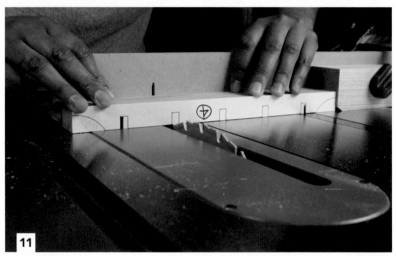

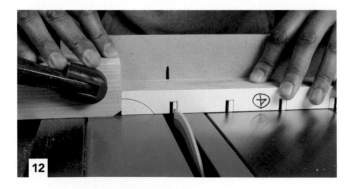

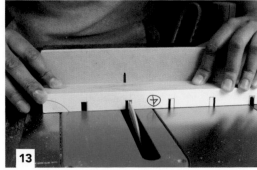

10. Make the first cut.
Most plywood is actually thinner than the stated thicknesses, so it is best to use a single saw blade instead of a stack dado blade in this instance. A couple of cuts will need to be made to widen each notch. Proceed to make the first cut in the first notch. Then, flip the runners end for end to complete the opposite end.

11. Prepare and cut the second notch.
After the end notches have received their first cuts, adjust the stop block to set up for the inside notches. Notice the location of the stop block. Flip the runners end for end to complete the opposite notch. After the first cuts have been made on the two exterior notches, remove the stop block to make the first cut in the center notch. No need to set up the stop block here, since there is only one center notch.

12. Widen the notches.
When you have completed the first cuts on all notches, set up the stop block to widen the notches. Line up the blade with the marks you made earlier. Make the second cut to widen the notch. Flip the runners end for end to complete the end notches.

13. Complete each notch.
It is a good idea to have an extra runner cut to use as a test piece to test fit the notches. After you have completed the end notches, finish widening the remaining notches using the same method as used earlier.

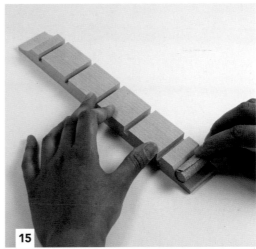

14. Cut out the profile.
When all of the notches are complete, proceed to cut out the end profiles of the runners. Use the scroll saw equipped with a bigger blade to complete the cut.

15. Sand the profile.
Before separating the runners, use a ½" (13mm)-diameter dowel wrapped with various grits of sandpaper to sand the profile to a smooth finish. Separate the runners and sand all other edges while maintaining square.

16. Cut the notches in the panels.
Transfer the thickness of the runners onto the bottom edge of one panel. Use these lines to set up the table saw to cut shallow ⅛" (3mm)-high corresponding notches in all the panels. These shallow notches will fit into the notches made earlier on the runners. We are essentially creating a lap joint.

17. Apply a finish.
The beauty of this file holder is that it can be taken apart when not in use. So, due to the strong lap joint, there is no need for glue here. Apply a clear protective spray finish to all parts of the file holder. Work in a well-ventilated area and wear an organic vapor respirator.

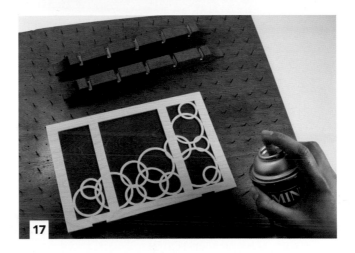

koi file organizer

The alternate pattern I have designed for this project is a variation of the stylized koi fish design, as discussed in the four squares wall art project (page 96). I simply uncurled the fish and added some swaying reeds to convey depth and a sense of movement.

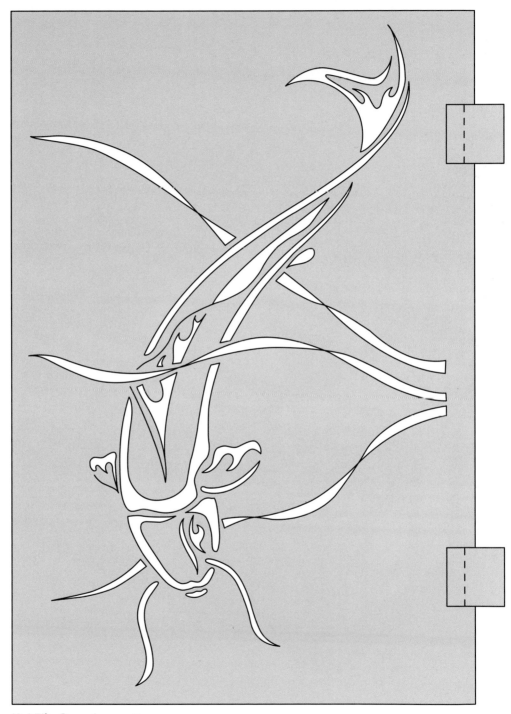

Runner

Koi File Organizer pattern
Make 1 copy at 125%

tissue box cover

TOOLS & MATERIALS

- Table saw
- Drill press
- Drill bits (various sizes)
- Scroll saw blades, reverse tooth #2 and #5
- Wood glue
- White glue
- Glue brush
- Glue roller
- Spray adhesive
- Sandpaper (various grits)
- Sanding block
- Clamps
- Double-sided tape
- Clear packing tape
- Painter's masking tape
- Stain/dye of choice (optional)
- Shallow container
- Finish of choice
- Scrap backer material
- Fine tip marker
- Nonslip bumper pads or felt pads (optional)

Every office needs a box of tissues. As I am writing this I find myself reaching for a tissue every 5 minutes. I love my cats, but my nose feels differently. I wanted to disguise the often-unattractive cardboard box that the tissues come in. I ended up with a design that I am sure will fit into any decor from traditional to modern. The pattern is a variation of the cubic design as seen in the picture frame project (page 64). The versatility of these patterns enables you to create a fabulous set of matching home décor pieces. The tissue box cover is made for a standard tissue box. Simply make adjustments to the size and pattern if you prefer the bigger boxes. The tissue box cover consists of 2 sub-assemblies—the inner box and the outer wrap. Both assemblies have simple mitered joinery, which was also cut on the table saw. The outer wrap parts will be stained before it is assembled and attached to the inner assembly. Never have sniffly days looked so good!

CUTTING LIST

	Part #	Amount	Part Name	Measurement	Material
Inner Assembly:	1	1	Top	¼" x 5" x 9½" (6mm x 127mm x 241mm)	Plywood
	2	2	Sides	¼" x 3⅛" x 9½" (6mm x 79mm x 241mm)	Plywood
	3	2	Ends	¼" x 3⅛" x 5¼" (6mm x 79mm x 133mm)	Plywood
Outer Assembly:	4	1	Top	⅛" x 5¼" x 9½" (3mm x 133mm x 241mm)	Plywood
	5	2	Sides	¼" x 3¼" x 9¾" (6mm x 83mm x 248mm)	Plywood
	6	2	Ends	¼" x 3¼" x 5½" (6mm x 83mm x 140mm)	Plywood

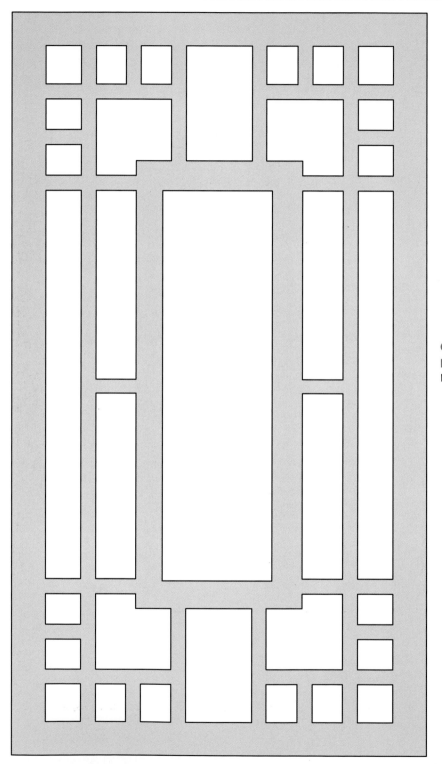

**Cubic Tissue Box Cover
pattern, Top, #4**
Make 1 copy at 125%

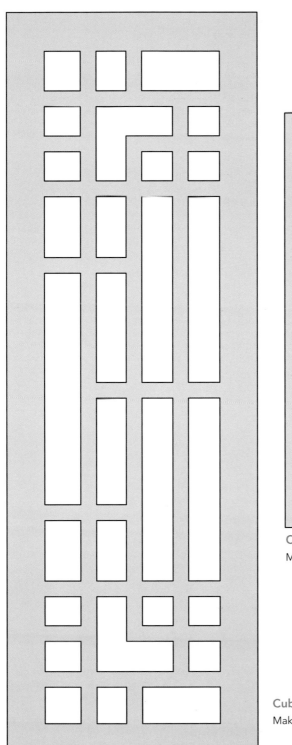

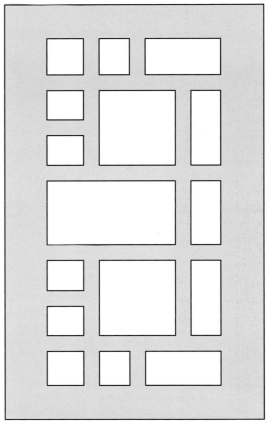

Cubic Tissue Box Cover pattern, Ends, #6
Make 1 copy at 125%

Cubic Tissue Box Cover pattern, Sides, #5
Make 1 copy at 125%

Cubic Tissue Cover Step-by-Step

1. Prepare the stock.
Cut/rip the sides and ends to the final width on the table saw with the blade set at 90° to the table. Use the table saw with the blade tilted at 45° to cut the miters on the sides and ends of the inner assembly. Use a stop block to get the exact same length on the corresponding parts. Leave extra width on outer assembly parts to be mitered at a later stage.

2. Number all parts.
Keep track of all the parts by numbering each part as they are cut. Always keep the cutting list handy to refer to as needed.

3. Glue the parts of the inner assembly.
Always perform a dry clamp of all parts to verify the fit before applying any glue. When you are satisfied with the fit, apply wood glue with a glue brush to all miters and clamp. Remember to check the assembly to see if it is square.

4. Prepare the outer assembly.
Now that the inner assembly is glued, proceed with cutting the miters on the outer assembly ends and sides. Cut a miter on one end of an end part and a side part first. Clamp the end part to the inner assembly, lining up the inside of the miter to the corner. Then, hold or clamp the miter of the side part against the miter of the end part and mark the length of the inner assembly onto the side part. This mark will be used to line up with the blade to miter the side part to final length. Repeat step for end parts.

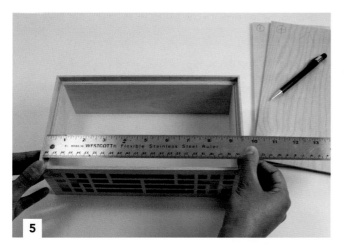

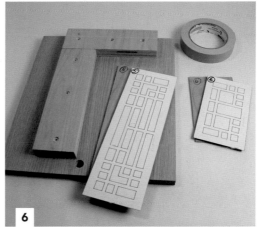

5. Measure for the top parts.
Temporarily attach the outer parts to the inner assembly with clear packing tape. We have created an instant rabbet. Now you can measure the exact width and length of the opening to prepare the top part.

6. Stack the outer assembly parts.
Use the right-angle alignment jig to stack the two ends together and then the two sides together. Make sure the paper patterns have been cut to exact dimensions and attached to their respective parts first. Also, ensure the parts are stacked with the miters facing down. Attach a scrap backer to the outer assembly top part.

7. Drill the blade entry holes.
With all the corresponding parts stacked, use the drill press to drill blade entry holes. Drill the holes as close to a corner or line as possible.

8. Cut out the pattern on the side and end parts.
To achieve nice, crisp inside corners on a square cutout, we first have to make rounded corners when scrolling. The obvious rounded corners I am creating are more for demonstration purposes. The rounded corners you scroll do not need to be so extreme. To complete the corners, simply go back and square each corner.

Cubic Tissue Cover Step-by-Step *(continued)*

9. Cut out the pattern on the top part.
Use the same method to cut out the pattern on the top part.
Be sure to leave the center opening for a later stage.

10. Attach the top parts.
With the aid of the right-angle alignment jig, temporarily attach
the top cutout part to the inner assembly top part. Mark each
corresponding corner for easy assembly at a later stage.

11. Cut out the center opening.
Drill a blade-entry hole in the corner of the opening. Cut out the
center opening using a #5 or bigger reverse-tooth blade. After the
opening is cut, do not separate parts just yet.

12. Temporarily attach all parts.
Use strips of double-sided tape to temporarily attach all parts.
Use clamp pressure to ensure the parts are well adhered.

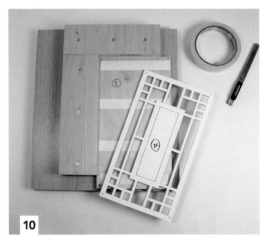

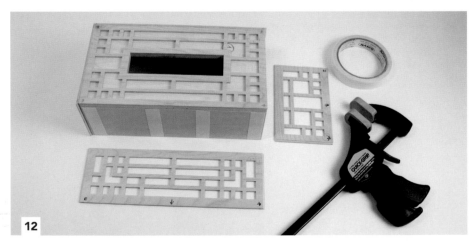

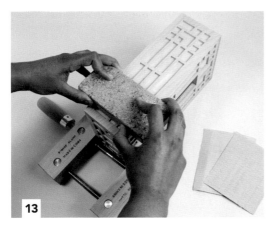

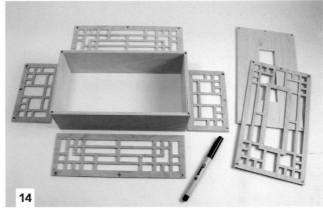

13. Sand all parts flush.
Use a sanding block with various grits of sandpaper to sand all sides flush. Use the sanding base with a full sheet of sandpaper to sand the bottom edges flush. Soften all edges with 220-grit sandpaper.

14. Mark all parts.
After everything is sanded flush, separate each part. Make sure to use a fine-tip marker to mark each corresponding part as they are separated. Indicate with an arrow which way is up on the cutouts. On the top parts, indicate with an X the interior surfaces to be glued together at a later stage.

15. Stain the cutouts.
Fill a shallow container with stain of your choice. Dip the clean cutouts into the stain. Use a shop-made drying rack made of toothpicks and a cork board to air dry each part.

16. Tape the ends.
After the stain is dry, tape all mitered ends together using clear packing tape. To help protect the finish from clear tape residue and prevent messy glue squeeze-out, apply painter's masking tape to the outside ends of the mitered parts first.

Cubic Tissue Cover Step-by-Step *(continued)*

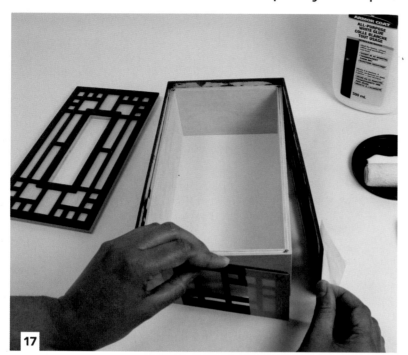

17. Glue the 2 assemblies together.
Use a glue roller to roll an even layer of white glue on the back of the cutouts. Wrap the cutouts around each corner of the inner assembly. Match each corresponding corner with the help of the indicating marks made earlier. Glue the top into the opening. Clamp the whole assembly.

18. Apply a finish.
After the glue is dry, elevate the tissue box cover using anything handy. Apply a few coats of a clear protective spray. Once dry, lightly scuff-sand between each coat.

Apply non-slip bumper pads or felt pads to the bottom of each corner to finish this project.

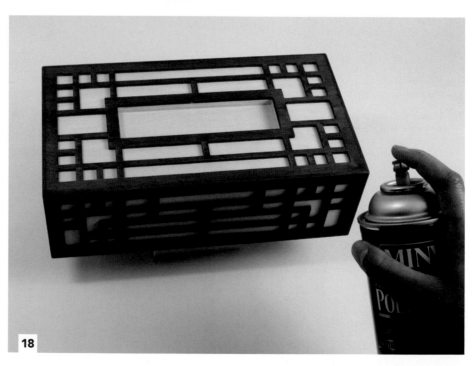

orchid tissue box cover

The alternate pattern I have designed for this project is a variation of the orchid design as seen in the picture frame project. Here, I have simply adapted the pattern by making it fit the horizontals of the sides, ends, and top of the tissue box cover.

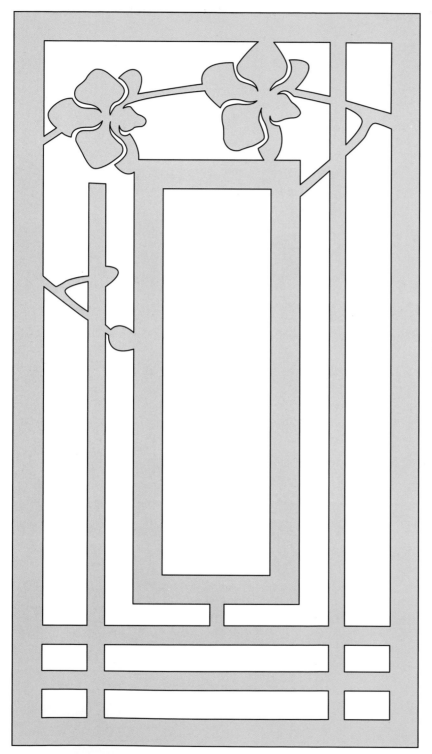

Orchid Tissue Box Cover pattern, Top, #4

Make 1 copy at 125%

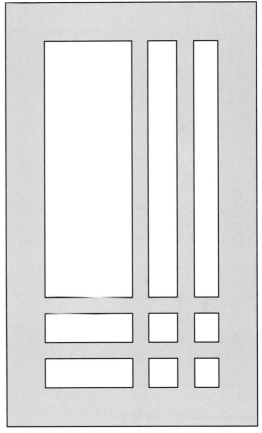

Orchid Tissue Box Cover pattern, Ends, #6
Make 1 copy at 125%

Orchid Tissue Box Cover pattern, Sides, #5
Make 1 copy at 125%

magnet board

TOOLS & MATERIALS

- Table saw
- Dado table saw blade (optional)
- Drill press
- Drill bit, ¹⁄₁₆" (2mm) diameter
- Scroll saw blades, reverse tooth #5 or choice
- Wood glue
- Contact cement (water-based)
- Polyurethane glue
- Spray adhesive glue
- Band clamps
- Clear packing tape
- Masking tape
- Sheet metal
- Tin snips
- Hammer
- Miter saw
- Screws #4, ½" (13mm) long
- Hand drill
- Iron
- Veneer tape (birch)
- Veneer J-roller
- Glue brush
- White glue
- Glue roller
- Utility knife
- Fine-tip red marker
- Watco Danish oil (or finish of choice)
- Sandpaper, 150 to 220 and 400 grit to 600 grit
- Blue paper towels or cotton rags
- Keyhole hangers
- Filler block, 4"x 4" (102mm x 102mm) plywood

The following project was an experiment that joined two very dissimilar materials. The problem was how to adhere wood to sheet metal without any visible fasteners. It's a matter of using the right adhesive for the right job. I used two types of adhesive in this project, which I will further discuss in the demonstration.

The materials used for this project include Finnish birch aircraft ply, as discussed in the bookmark project, and a sheet metal panel assembly that will give the wood its magnetic ability. The piece itself will consist of two individual frames, which when hung together reveal a stunning image. I do recommend that you obtain some rare earth magnets, which will have more holding power than the common sheet magnet found on many refrigerator magnets. Hanging this piece in your office will surely "attract" some welcome attention!

The pattern I chose to demonstrate is loosely based on a Celtic knot. I simply elongated the design, creating a tribal design effect.

CUTTING LIST

Part #	Amount	Part Name	Measurement	Material
1	2	Pattern panels	³⁄₃₂" x 12" x 12" (2.5mm x 305mm x 305mm)	Finnish birch
2	2	Metal backer panels	¹⁄₆₄" x 11¾" x 11¾" (.4mm x 298mm x 298mm)	Metal
3	2	Frame panels	¼" x 11¾" x 11¾" (6mm x 298mm x 298mm)	MDF
4	8	Frame members	⅜" x 1¼" x 12" (10mm x 32mm x 305mm)	Birch plywood

Knot Magnet Board pattern
Make 1 copy at 300%

Knot Magnet Board Step-by-Step

1. Prepare the stock.
Cut the frame sides to width on the table saw. Cut and miter the sides to final length by using the miter saw setup with a stop block since the sides are the same length.

2. Gather all parts.
Use the cutting list to make sure you have all the appropriate parts cut. Cut all parts, except the frame sides, a bit oversized—you will cut most parts to fit. Make sure you have a pair of tin snips to cut the metal backers to size.

3. Rabbet the frame sides.
Equip the table saw with a dado blade stacked to ¼" (6mm) wide. Clamp an auxiliary fence to your table saw fence since the fence will need to be right against the blade to achieve a ¼" (6mm)-wide by ¼" (6mm)-deep rabbet. If you do not have a dado set, use your single saw blade to cut, and continue to move and adjust the fence to make another cut until you reach ¼" (6mm) width.

4. Assemble the frames.
After all of the rabbets are cut to the right width and depth, use a glue brush to apply wood glue to all frame miters. Use either a band clamp or clear packing tape to clamp the corners in place.

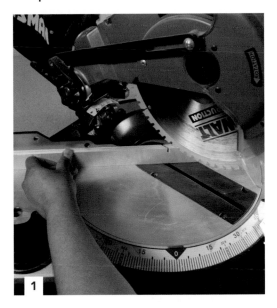

Knot Magnet Board Step-by-Step *(continued)*

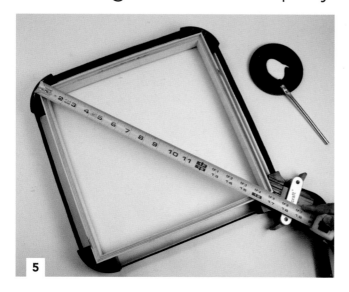

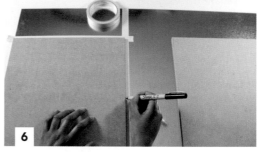

5. Check frames for square.
As soon as the frame is glued, check for square by measuring the diagonals from corner to corner. If you find that one diagonal is longer than the other, use a clamp across the longer diagonal to bring it to square.

6. Prepare the metal backing.
Determine the exact length and width of the medium-density fiberboard (MDF) frame panels by measuring the opening from one rabbet to the next. Cut the MDF panels to size. Use the MDF panel as a template to size the metal backers. Apply masking tape across the metal at roughly where the MDF will be, place the MDF on the masking tape, and draw the cut lines.

7. Cut the metal backer.
Cut the sheet metal to size using a pair of tin snips. Wear a good pair of work gloves when handling sheet metal. To avoid or minimize curls/ripples in the sheet metal, do not close the snips completely. Use shorter strokes/cuts, which will yield a smoother edge on the metal. Try to cut on the outside of the line so that the metal backer will overhang slightly on the MDF panel.

8. Smooth the cut metal edges.
You will notice that the cut metal backers will be slightly curled. To smooth these curls, gently hammer them down.

9. Glue the metal to the MDF panel.
Mark an X on the inside faces of the metal and MDF panels. Brush or spray the water-based contact cement on both surfaces. Work in a well-ventilated area. Wait until both surfaces become tacky to the touch. Place 2 strips of wood between the layers. As you align the metal to the MDF panel, remove one stick at a time. Use a veneer roller to press down firmly so that the 2 pieces fully adhere to one another. Because the metal panel slightly overhangs the MDF panel, flush them up with a metal file.

10. Glue panels to the frames.

Use a glue brush to spread some wood glue on the inside of the rabbets. Insert the metal panels into the opening of the frames and clamp in place.

11. Drill the blade-entry holes.

There is a top and bottom to this design, so the pieces cannot be stack cut. Keep track of the top and bottom by marking them. Attach each panel to a scrap backer with masking tape. Use a ¹⁄₁₆" (2mm) drill bit in the drill press to drill the blade-entry holes. Sand away any burrs left on the back of the panels.

12. Cut out the pattern.

Cut out the pattern using a #5 reverse-tooth blade. Cut out the smaller parts first and leave the larger cutouts for later. For crisp, sharp corners, round the corners first and then go back to square it up.

13. Cut out the shape of the pattern.

Since the pattern lines are just guides, it is best to adjust the size of the panel accordingly. Trace the outline of the frame assembly onto the cutout panel with a fine tip red marker. Now, cut out the outline of the panel using a straight edge and a utility knife.

10

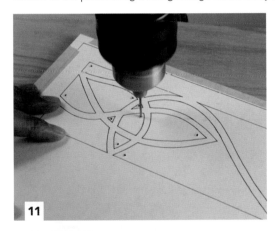

11

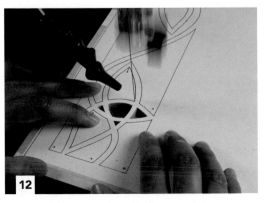

12

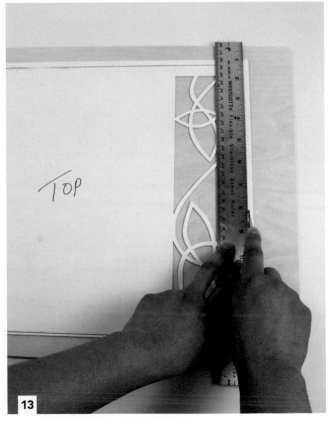

13

Knot Magnet Board Step-by-Step *(continued)*

14. Glue the cutout panel to the frame assembly.
Use a thin piece of scrap wood or hard plastic to spread a thin layer of polyurethane glue (or any glue that is formulated to bond wood to metal) on the back of the cutouts. This glue cures with the presence of moisture, so spray some water onto the metal before clamping the pieces together.

15. Clamp the assembly.
With the use of two clamping blocks, a.k.a. ¾" (19mm)-thick wood scraps, carefully clamp the cutout to the frame. Use some masking tape to keep the cutout aligned to the frame while the assembly is being clamped. After the glue is dry, remove the paper pattern and lightly sand the entire magnet board to a smooth finish.

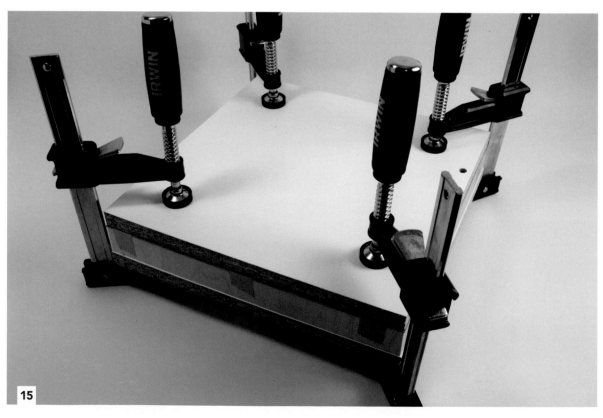

16. Attach the keyhole wall hanger.
You will need a filler block that sits flush to the edge of the frame. My blocks are approximately 4" x 4" (102mm x 102mm). Find the center of the top edge of the frame and the filler block. Glue the block to the frame by lining up the center lines. Draw the outline of the hanger on center. (See Layered Wall Art, page 126, for more instructions.) You will need a ⅝" and ⅜" (16mm and 10mm)-diameter Forstner bit to drill the appropriate recess holes.

17. Apply a finish.
Apply a couple of coats of oil finish to the completed magnet board. Use a towel to apply the first coat, and wet-dry 400- to 600-grit sandpaper to rub in the subsequent coats. The magnet boards are now sure to attract some attention!

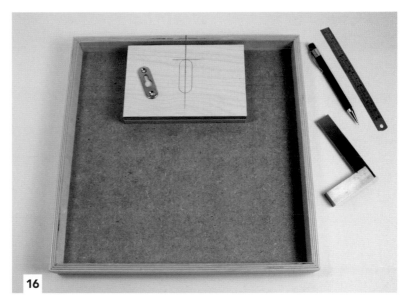

16

17

cherry blossom magnet board

The alternate pattern for this project is a delicate cherry blossom silhouette. The cherry blossom has many symbolic meanings for different cultures, including love, power, and because it blooms only for a short time, the impermanence of life. I have divided the cherry blossom motif across the two framed panels of the magnet board. When the two panels are brought together, it will reveal one dynamic unified piece.

**Cherry Blossom
Magnet Board pattern**
Make 1 copy at 300%

appendix

Throughout the book you will notice that I use several jigs to aid in the efficient construction of each project. In this section, I will show you how to construct these simple yet effective jigs with step-by-step instructions. I will start by showing you how to make a very easy and efficient edge sander, which will make the sanding process less tedious. Since most of the projects depend on accuracy, to aid in the precise stacking of parts, I will also provide step-by-step instructions on a very useful right-angle alignment jig. To provide strength and beauty to mitered corners, I will show you how to construct a very easy table saw spline slot cutting jig. All these jigs will prove to be invaluable additions to your workshop. I've also included the other 11 Chinese zodiac patterns for the bookmark project on page 42.

The edge-sanding jig.

The right-angle alignment jig.

Slot-cutting table saw jig.

edge-sanding jig

This jig was born out of my need for a quick and accurate sanding aid that would make the sanding of edges and ends a snap, while maintaining squareness. Just make sure the parts of the jig are square and true. A machinist square, commonly known as a steel square, is a great precision tool to lead you in the right direction.

TOOLS & MATERIALS

- Table saw
- Hand drill
- Drill bits and countersink
- Wood screws, #6, ¼" (6mm)
- Double-sided tape
- Steel square
- Spray adhesive glue
- Sandpaper (grit of choice)
- Clamps

CUTTING LIST

Part #	Amount	Part Name	Measurement	Material
1	1	Base	⅝" x 6½" x 12" (16mm x 165mm x 305mm)	Plywood/MDF
2	1	Edging strip	⅝" x 2½" x 12" (16mm x 64mm x 305mm)	Plywood/MDF

Edge-Sanding Jig Step-by-Step

1. Prepare the stock.
Use a table saw to cut the parts to final length and width. To ensure the base and the edge strip are the same length, clamp a stop block to the miter gauge of the table saw. Make sure that all the parts have nice square corners, edges, and ends. Check for square by using a steel square.

2. Chamfer the edge of the base.
As the base will be butted up against the edge strip, and it's likely that the corner will get clogged with sanding dust, chamfer the inside top corner of the base. Now all you have to do is give the channel a brush occasionally.

3. Drill holes into the edge strip.
Transfer the thickness of the base onto the outside face of the edge strip. Mark and drill four evenly spaced countersink holes on center. Use a scrap backer board to prevent tear out on the edge strip.

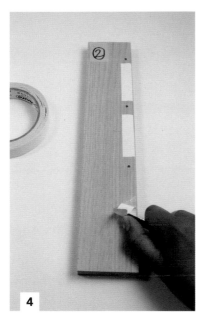

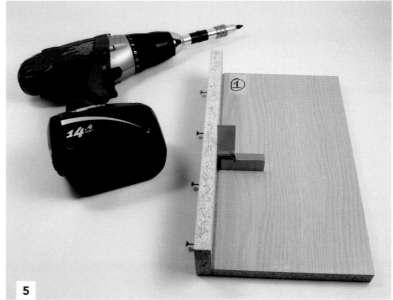

4

5

4. Apply double-sided tape to edge strip.

To help keep the parts in place when attaching the screws, apply a few strips of double-sided tape to the inside face of the edge strip. Do not allow the tape to go beyond the top of the base. Line up the ends of the parts and press together; apply clamp pressure to fully adhere. Remove the clamp promptly.

5. Attach the edge strip to the base.

With an appropriate drill bit, drill pilot holes into the base through the countersink holes made earlier. Place a steel square in the corner of the assembly to check for square. Continue to check for square as you drive the screws into the base.

6. Cut and glue sandpaper to the jig.

Cut a strip of the desired grit of sandpaper. Apply spray adhesive to the back of the strip. Seat the bottom edge of the strip in the channel created by the chamfer of the base and apply some pressure. When you want to change a used strip, simply remove and apply a new one.

6

right-angle alignment jig

I wanted to take the guesswork out of accurately aligning parts when stacking. Since most of the projects depend on this accuracy, I came up with a simple and very efficient right-angle alignment jig. It is a snap to construct and all you need are shop wood scraps. Just make sure that the parts are square and true.

TOOLS & MATERIALS

- Table saw
- Hand drill
- Drill bits and countersink
- Wood screws #6, 1¼" (32mm)
- Double-sided tape
- Set square
- Sandpaper or edge-sanding jig
- Clamps

CUTTING LIST

Part #	Amount	Part Name	Measurement	Material
1	1	Base	⅝" x 10" x 12" (16mm x 254mm x 305mm)	Plywood/MDF
2	1	Vertical strip	¾" x 2" x 8½" (19mm x 51mm x 216mm)	Plywood/MDF
3	1	Horizontal strip	¾" x 2" x 7" (19mm x 51mm x 178mm)	Plywood/MDF

Right-angle Alignment Jig Step-by-Step

1. Prepare the stock.
Use a table saw to cut the parts. Cut the horizontal strip shorter than the vertical strip. Lay out evenly spaced marks on the center on both strips to receive #6, 1¼" (32mm) screws at a later stage.

2. Drill holes in the strips.
Use a quick-change bit set to drill countersink screw holes. The beauty of this bit set is that you can easily change from a drill bit to a driver bit, simply by flipping the bit set end-for-end in the holder.

3. Chamfer the corner of the vertical strip.
Use our newly made edge sander to chamfer the inside corner of the vertical strip. The chamfer will prevent any burrs on a piece of wood from throwing off the alignment of the stack.

4. Apply double-sided tape to the edge strip.
As previously demonstrated in the edge-sanding jig project, place a few strips of double-sided tape on the underside of both strips. This will help hold the pieces in place when they're being screwed to the base.

5. Attach the strips to the base.
Align the horizontal strip to the top edge of the base approximately 1" (25mm) in from the right side of the base. Align the vertical strip to the end of the horizontal strip. Use a square to keep the parts square and press them into place. Apply clamp pressure. Keep the square in place as you drill pilot holes. Apply screws.

slot-cutting table saw jig

This is a simple jig for the table saw that will yield beautiful results. This spline slot-cutting jig is an effective tool to supply much-needed strength to mitered corners. It is my preferred joinery method, not only for strength, but beauty as well. A corner of a frame or box has never looked this good!

TOOLS & MATERIALS

- Table saw
- Miter saw
- Air nailer and nails (optional)
- Clamps
- Wood glue
- Steel square
- Hand drill
- Drill bits and countersink
- Wood screws #6, 1¼" (32mm)
- Sandpaper

CUTTING LIST

Part #	Amount	Part Name	Measurement	Material
1	1	Base	¾" x 8½" x 12½" (19mm x 216mm x 318mm)	Plywood/MDF
2	2	Cradle strip	¾" x 3" x 8½" (19mm x 76mm x 216mm)	Plywood/MDF

Slot-Cutting Table Saw Jig Step-By-Step

1. Prepare the stock.
Use a table saw to cut the parts to final length and width. To ensure the base and the edge strip are the same length, clamp a stop block to the miter gauge of the table saw. Make sure that all parts have nice square corners, edges, and ends. Check for square, using a steel square.

2. Cut the miters on cradle strips.
Cut a miter at the bottom end of each strip. You can cut it on the table saw with a blade tilted to 45°, but it is more convenient to cut on the miter saw.

3. Mark the thickness of the first strip.
Locate the first strip about 2¼" (57mm) down from the top edge of the base. Find the center of the base and place the first strip with the miter flush to the bottom edge of the base. Use a square block to make sure the parts are flush. Hold the strip in place and mark its thickness on the base.

4. Glue the first strip.
Apply a bead of wood glue within the layout lines. Reposition the first strip and clamp in place. To speed up the process, you can shoot a few brad nails into the back. Clamp the piece with quick clamps.

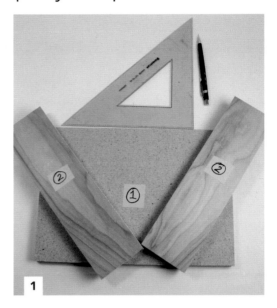

1

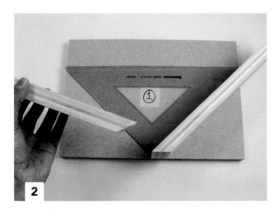

2

3

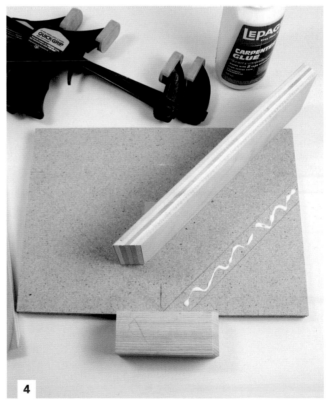

4

Slot-Cutting Table Saw Jig Step-By-Step *(continued)*

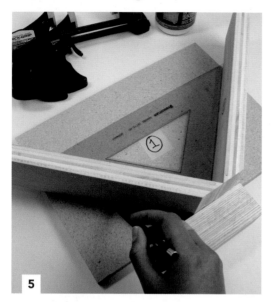

5. Mark the second strip.
Once the glue is dry on the first piece, you can now place the second strip in position. Use the square to position the second piece in place. Flush up the miter to the bottom edge of the base. Hold down and mark the thickness onto the base.

6. Glue the second strip.
Apply a few beads of glue within the layout lines of the second strip. Once the piece is in place, slide the strip up and down to get some of the glue onto the strip. Reposition using the square. Clamp in place. Check that the strips are square to the base.

7. Mark the thickness of the strips on the back.
When the glue is dry, use your combination square to transfer the thickness of the strips onto the back of the base. These lines will give you the exact location of the strips for attaching the base with screws.

8. Screw strips to the base.
Use a hand drill to make countersink holes, evenly spaced and on center through the base into the strips. Use #6, 1¼" (32mm)-long screws to secure the pieces together. Sand any burrs around the countersink holes.

more bookmark patterns

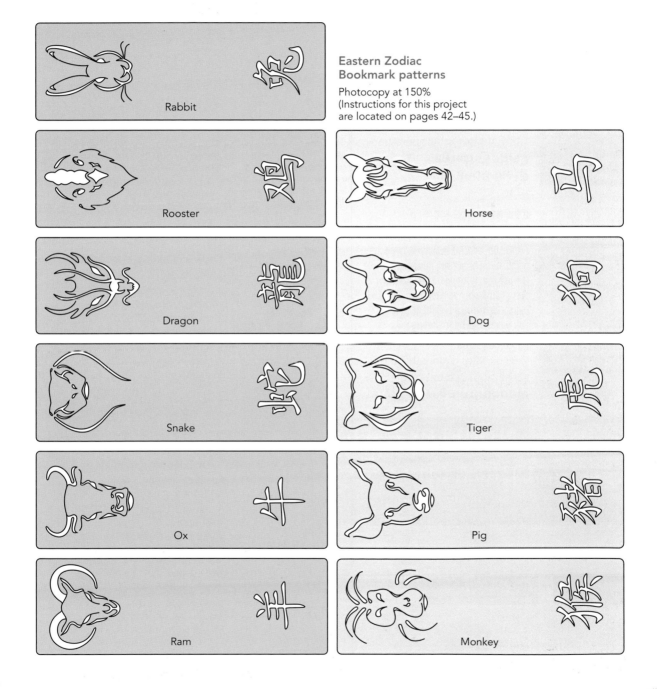

**Eastern Zodiac
Bookmark patterns**

Photocopy at 150%
(Instructions for this project
are located on pages 42–45.)

Rabbit

Rooster

Horse

Dragon

Dog

Snake

Tiger

Ox

Pig

Ram

Monkey

index

Note: Page numbers in bold indicate projects.

ACQUISITION EDITOR
Peg Couch

COPY EDITOR
Paul Hambke

COVER AND LAYOUT DESIGNER
Lindsay Hess

EDITORIAL ASSISTANTS
Liz Norris and Heather Stauffer

EDITOR
Kerri Landis

GALLERY PHOTOGRAPHER
Scott Kriner

PROOFREADER
Lynda Jo Runkle

INDEXER
Jay Kreider

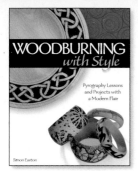

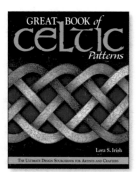
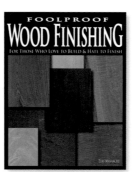